W9-BAL-758

Madame Jeanne Guyon

CHILD OF ANOTHER WORLD

Madame Jeanne Guyon

CHILD OF ANOTHER WORLD

Dorothy Gawne Coslet

CLC PUBLICATIONS
Fort Washington, PA 19034

Published by CLC ∘ Publications

U.S.A.
P.O. Box 1449, Fort Washington, PA 19034

GREAT BRITAIN
51 The Dean, Alresford, Hants. SO24 9BJ

AUSTRALIA
P.O. Box 419M, Manunda, QLD 4879

NEW ZEALAND
10 MacArthur Street, Feilding

Copyright © 1984
Dorothy Gawne Coslet

All Rights Reserved

ISBN 0-87508-144-4

Excerpts from *Madame Guyon, an Autobiography* by
Moody Press, Moody Bible Institute of Chicago.
Used by permission.

Excerpts from *The Life and Religious Opinions of Madame Guyon*
by Thomas G. Upham, Allenson and Co., Ltd., London, England,
and James Clark and Co., Ltd., All Saints Passage,
Cambridge, England. Used by permission.

This printing 2002

Printed in the United States of America

Contents

Introduction

This biography of Madame Jeanne Guyon (1648-1717) will introduce you to a woman who was. . .

- deeply in love with her Savior. . .
- greatly used of God to bless and challenge Christians through her writings . . .
- widely misunderstood and hated because of her fervent yet simple faith . . .
- doggedly persecuted as a heretic by authorities of her beloved Roman Catholic Church.

You will also come to understand what it was that motivated this French noblewoman and kept her faithful to her unpopular beliefs despite her unsettled childhood, loveless marriage and early widowhood. It is our desire and prayer that you too, the reader, will be brought closer to the Lord Jesus as you are inspired by this true drama of a woman who understood the cost, and the ecstacy, of the words: "*For me to live is Christ, and to die is gain.*"

Mrs. Coslet, who ably writes this account, holds a Master of Theology degree from American Bible College and Divinity School and is a graduate of the Famous Writers School. She resides in Helena, Montana.

—*The Publishers*

1

God's Call

The hired boat pushed away from the dock. Slowly it moved up the River Seine, unnoticed. On board were the young, recently widowed Madame Jeanne Guyon, her five-year-old daughter and three women companions. Huddling together in the darkness, the women felt confident that no one on the dock had recognized Madame Guyon or any of her traveling party. After all, they were well disguised by all the clothing they'd put on to avoid carrying so much personal luggage onto the boat.

All was quiet and still, that warm, stuffy July 1681 night—just the way they had prayed it would be. As they crept along, the waves slapped the sides of the boat. The smallest sounds seemed to amplify the loud pounding of their own hearts and the darkness of the night. Crickets chirped on the nearby shore. A dog barked in the distance, But, thanks be to God, there were no sounds of approaching soldiers.

Madame Guyon left Paris that night assured of one thing—that God had a ministry for her.

She had decided to set out secretly on this boat rather than take the stagecoach on which she had booked passage, so that she and her friends could be far away before Father La Mothe learned of their whereabouts. Even though she was his half-sister, La Mothe had threatened to expose her religious views to the judgment of Church authorities and was determined to prevent her from going to Switzerland on what he termed a foolhardy adventure. But Madame Guyon was all the more determined to go.

If this be truly the will of God for me at this time, she reasoned within herself, *I must go!*

The circumstances leading up to this woman's hasty departure had begun months before. Early that spring, while Madame Guyon was in Paris on business, she went to a church. There she approached the first confessor-priest she found in the building and for a while sat in the dimly lit confessional booth in silence. Since Madame Guyon was not acquainted with the resident clergy in this church, we can safely assume, as did she, that this priest did not know her by sight and therefore had no intimate knowledge of her religious experience and personal commitment to the Lord Jesus Christ. How surprised she was when the priest said, "Although I do not know who you are, I do feel strongly led to exhort you to do what the Lord has made known to you. That He requires of you. That is all I have to say."

"But Father," she replied, "I am a widow with three young children to raise. This is a full-time job in itself. What more could God require of me except to look after them during their formative years?"

"I know nothing about these particulars, my good lady," responded the priest. "You know that if God shows to you that He requires something of you, there is absolutely nothing in the world which ought to hinder you from doing His will. Even if you must leave your children to accomplish it, the sacrifice is necessary. There can be no excuse."

Madame Guyon returned to her home in Montargis, a small village some fifty miles south of Paris, convinced in her own heart that she must obey God's voice and heed the Lord's call even though she did not understand thoroughly what God expected of her. The admonition of this confessor-priest confirmed her calling. She was aware that it could mean personal inconvenience and sacrifice. But what about her children? They were so young and had no father. Must they suffer the loss of a mother also? Sometimes she clung to the hope that surely God would not ask such a sacrifice of her. Perhaps this was only a test of loyalty to prove her faith. Perhaps God might only want her to endow a hospital . . . or donate money to a group of New Catholics for the establishment of a school in Geneva. Was this what God was really saying? If so, she could do this good work for God and the Church and still stay with her little family. But what did this have to do with Geneva, Switzerland? That city, she knew, was populated mostly by Protestant Calvinists who had left the Roman Catholic Church to follow the teachings of the heretic John Calvin. Surely, as a devout Catholic, she had no intention of leaving the Church of her baptism.

Agreeing with this confessor-priest in Paris to submit herself to whatever the Lord required, Madame Guyon decided to tell no one about hearing the voice of God. But why was it that Geneva had now come to her mind? Being called of God and yet not knowing what He expected her to do caused her great inner conflict. But try as she might, she could not rid herself of this concern for Geneva. Neither could she forget the Lord's words which she had heard even while her husband was yet alive: "What! Do you seek for ease and to shake off My all-powerful yoke?"

So she went home wracked by irresolution, hesitating to step in either direction until the hand of the Lord should show her His way more fully. But now she was assured of one thing: the question foremost in her heart was finally answered. God did have a ministry for her somewhere—and she must find it!

She finally did confide in her half-brother, Father La Mothe, other co-religionists and a few friends. But the idea that she was called by God into a place of ministry was looked upon with suspicion and doubt. One young clergyman told Madame Guyon quite frankly that even the *thought* of such a thing was a rash, ill-advised scheme bordering on insanity; worse still, it might be something contrived by Lucifer himself to tempt her. Her half-brother Father La Mothe and other well-meaning friends expressed much the same opinion. Bishop D'Aranthon, Mother Marie, Prioress of the New Catholics in Paris, Father Claude Martin, Monsieur Bertot and even Father La Combe, her spiritual director, reacted negatively to her concern for a ministry in Geneva. A few of them felt her call was genuine but suggested that she fulfill her mission without leaving France, by working with the poor and the handicapped.

The chaplain-priest to the Guyon household, on the other hand, offered her no encouragement whatever. In fact, he agreed with her half-brother completely. It was a foolish scheme, a serious error in judgment on her part, he concluded. He judged her alleged calling to be a product of her vivid imagination, a preoccupation that had grown within her during the tumultuous period of grief and boredom after the loss of her husband.

But the final confirmation of God's call came with the receipt of two letters from priests who lived nowhere near one another. They arrived almost simultaneously and contained practically the same message. Surely this was more than a coincidence.

In the first letter, Father Claude Martin wrote that, after much prayer, the Lord had now revealed to him that Madame Guyon must go to Geneva and make a willing sacrifice of everything to Him. The second letter came from Father Francois La Combe, her assigned spiritual director. He expressed much the same sentiments as had Father Martin. After praying much about her quandary, Father La Combe felt assured that the Lord wanted Madame Guyon to serve Him in Geneva and to do His will, whatever that might be.

Perhaps the Lord really requires of me nothing more than to endow a Church-related institution in Geneva, thought Madame Guyon. *This would be a worthy gesture. It would certainly be in God's will to have His work supported. And even a generous contribution would cause only a minor drain on my resources.*

She wrote the details of this thinking to Father Martin, explaining that her inherited wealth from her late husband, Monsieur Jacques Guyon, was more than sufficient to provide adequately for her family needs and still allow her to support her favorite charities. But Father Martin did not see it this way. He felt strongly about what the Lord had revealed to him and was sure that the Blessed Savior wanted her personal commitment, not just her worldly substance.

Finally she came to a decision. Nothing on earth would delay her now. Of course, doubts and fears were still there. It was unusual in those days for women to feel called of God, except to become a nun. But Madame Guyon vowed she would question God's will no longer.

Her mind was made up. She would go to Geneva regardless of the censure of those who meant well but did not understand the sincerity of her call.

What troubled her the most was her children's welfare. The thought of leaving them in the care of others saddened her. To think of putting them in boarding school or with foster parents was a heart-rending solution, but one that had to be considered. What had to be, had to be. Her dedication to Jesus Christ had to come first—even before her own dear children. But leaving them, she knew, would not be easy.

Preparations for the trip took longer than expected because they had to be accomplished without arousing suspicion. Then too, every circumstance that might occur in Madame Guyon's absence had to be considered and proper arrangements made. The administering of her late husband's investments, properties and business, besides the matter of providing for her mother-in-law and the three children, had to be settled in consultation with the family's legal advisor. All this took time.

Throughout her twelve years of marriage to Monsieur Jacques Guyon, Madame Jeanne Guyon had put up with the critical, rude ways of her mother-in-law, who shared their home. As soon as Jacques and Jeanne were married, Jacques' mother had purposely set about to irritate and try her new daughter-in-law's patience. She went so far as to prompt the household servants to do likewise. In order to maintain her Christian composure and to relieve her inner hurt, Jeanne could do little more than shut her eyes and ears to what was happening. She forced herself to think about the things of the Lord and to recite Scripture passages rapidly to herself. She filled her daytime hours with charitable works and found comfort in helping others. However, her mother-in-law never ceased to find fault with what Jeanne did; she reported Jeanne's generosity to Jacques. After receiving this complaint from his mother, Jacques required his wife to give a written account of all expenditures for household necessities, personal purchases, and contributions to the poor and to the Church. This was, he said, so that he could judge if she wisely used the allowance he had graciously given her.

During the 1680-81 winter, the last winter Madame Jeanne Guyon spent at home with her family, France had its most miserable and severe weather. Bitter cold, wind and heavy snow left the people cold, hungry and sick, especially in the larger cities. Wealthy families like the Guyons felt it their Christian duty to alleviate hunger and suffering by helping the poor insofar as they were able. So it was during these months of working together to help those less fortunate with bread, clothing, quilts and employment that the young widow and her mother-in-law came to appreciate one another.

How wonderful it was to have this closeness of heart and soul after all their years of bitterness and misunderstanding. Oh, if only this had happened sooner! Things might have been so different! As a result of spending that last winter together in the family mansion and their mutual concern for the welfare of others, this mother-in-law and her widowed daughter-in-law became united in love and affection where none had existed before. Now, as the date of Madame Guyon's planned departure neared, she realized it would not be as easy to leave since she and her elderly mother-in-law were on such good terms. More than once she thought, *How can I leave now?* Nevertheless, she had to do the Lord's work. As the days passed, the older Madame Guyon discovered she did not want her daughter-in-law to leave either. Now she could not do enough for Jeanne and her children.

In spite of her decision to follow the Lord's call, there were still times when Madame Guyon questioned her own faith. Could it be possible, after all, that she might be mistaken concerning the call of God in her life?

From the day of her conversion, the Lord Jesus Christ had been very real and near. His promise, "Lo, I am with you always," she accepted as hers. Now these words from the book of Isaiah came to her mind: "Fear not, . . . I will help thee, saith the Lord and thy Redeemer, the Holy One of Israel. . . . Fear not: for I have redeemed thee, I have called thee by thy name; thou art Mine. When thou passest through the waters, I will be with thee."

What reassuring words!

In the years that followed, God's holy presence became known to her in a most intimate way, fueling the inner fires of her soul to greater lengths of perseverance. Questions and doubts faded into the shadows, thereby confirming the validity of her call as the Holy Spirit had already revealed it to her. There was no turning back! The vows of her sacred marriage to the Lord Jesus Christ, her Blessed Savior, obligated her to follow Him wherever it was His pleasure and purpose to take her.

. . . . .

"Thou knowest, O my Beloved, that it was not the dread of Thy chastisements that sunk so deep, either into my understanding or my heart; it was the sorrow for offending Thee which ever constituted the whole of my distress, which was so great. I imagine that if there were neither heaven nor hell, I should always have retained the same innate fear of displeasing Thee. Thou knowest that after my faults, when, in all-forgiving mercy, Thou wert pleased to visit my soul, Thy caresses were a thousandfold more insupportable than Thy rod."

—Madame Jeanne Guyon

2

Early Childhood

Born on April 18, 1648, and baptized into the Roman Catholic Church on May 24 of that same year, Jeanne Marie Bouvieres de La Mothe, a sickly premature baby, was not expected to survive the hazards of early life. She continued to be frail and sickly all through childhood, sometimes but a heartbeat ahead of death itself.

Her father, Claude Bouvieres de La Mothe, a deeply religious man, was well-to-do and highly respected in the community. His title, Seigneur (Lord) de La Mothe Vergonville, indicates that at one time his family belonged to the aristocracy of France. He held a prestigious position similar to that of mayor in Montargis, in that part of France known before the French Revolution as the Province of Oreleanais.

Her mother, whose first name is not recorded anywhere, was a proud woman who disliked other women, including her daughters. She was not particularly religious. It was unfortunate that Madame Bouvieres de La Mothe was more concerned with social affairs and charities than she was in the upbringing of her children. She found many activities more challenging than hearth and home. So the servants and the older children looked after little Jeanne Marie most of the time.

Both her father and mother had been previously married. The father had a son and a daughter; the mother, a daughter. Little Jeanne Marie found herself being watched over, pushed around, loved and corrected by these older children, especially by her half-brother, who enjoyed bossing her around the most.

It was this apparent lack of maternal affection that led Monsieur Bouvieres de La Mothe to place this youngest daughter, Jeanne Marie, in the nearby Ursuline Seminary when she was but a two-and-a-half-year-old toddler. A bit too young for the disciplined life there, Jeanne Marie responded remarkably well to the personal attention and affection of the nuns to whom she was assigned. After about six months she returned home. But things were no different there.

Late in 1652 the Duchess of Montbason, a friend of the de La Mothe family, came to reside with the Benedictine nuns there. She persuaded Monsieur de La Mothe to enroll his pretty, petite, four-year-old Jeanne Marie in the Convent of the Benedictines. Here, he felt confident, the child would get the care and attention her mother seemed unable to give. At the convent Jeanne Marie became like a little shadow to the magnificent Duchess who looked after her.

Thus it was, while living in daily association with the Benedictine nuns, the Duchess and the young girls in the convent, that Jeanne Marie saw many good examples of Christian behavior which she tried to imitate.

How delighted she was when given the privilege of wearing a nun's habit. Even at this young age she had some very traumatic religious experiences and expressed a desire to lead a religious life insofar as would be expected of a child. She loved the Lord Jesus with all her heart and found satisfaction in the rituals of ceremonial worship in the chapel services.

One night Jeanne Marie had a frightening dream about hell. Upon seeing this horrible dark place where condemned souls are tormented and punished forever for their earthly transgressions, she realized that hell was just as real as the nuns had said it was. Because she was often reprimanded for her childish behavior, Jeanne Marie could not help but think that such a punishment as hell was intended for her. Overwhelmed by this vivid dream and the reality of hell, she cried, "Oh, my God, if Thou wilt have mercy upon me, and spare me yet a little longer, I will never again offend Thee."

Fearful lest she should close her eyes and die unforgiven and wake up in hell, she insisted upon making confession that very moment. Because she was such a young child, she was not permitted to go to the confessional booth alone. She still needed guidance in such matters. So a nun accompanied her and remained while the priest listened to her lengthy confession. How astonished the nun was! Even the priest laughed at first when she told him, in her sincere, childish way, that she had some doubts about the Roman Catholic faith and Church doctrine! She confessed being skeptical of the nuns' description of hell. She had supposed the nuns warned the girls about hell with all its horror and never-ending punishments only to make the girls more obedient and submissive to convent rules. But after seeing the place in her dream, she had panicked.

"Now I believe it. I do, I do believe it," she sobbed.

In making this confession she realized as never before that even though she was only five years old, she was a wicked sinner in need of salvation. She begged the priest for Christ's forgiveness and abso-lution of her sins. Most serious in her intentions to please God and also to escape the torments of hell, Jeanne Marie wanted to purge her soul of every dark and ugly sin, known and unknown, to be sure of her soul's salvation.

Since her tendency was to be open and frank with the older girls in the convent, Jeanne Marie did not hesitate to tell them about her experiences. She even mentioned that she desired to do some-thing for God—like being a Christian martyr—to prove her love and devotion to the Blessed Savior.

When the older girls heard of the child's desire, they were excited. To Jeanne Marie this was an ex-pression of her inward devotion to Christ and the Church. But to the other girls it presented another opportunity to tease the young child who was al-ready the butt of many of their ill-conceived jokes. They devised a scheme to convince Jeanne Marie that it was really the will of Almighty God that she become a Christian martyr right then. They assured her that when she was martyred she would go to heaven immediately and would enjoy God's holy presence forever. Hell would be banished from her, they said, once she sacrificed herself for Jesus' cause.

Much to their delight Jeanne Marie believed everything the older girls said. Of course she would be most happy to prove her loyalty and devotion to Jesus. The prospect of being a Christian martyr inspired her with faith and courage! Obviously she did not realize what martyrdom involved. Or perhaps she looked upon martyrdom symbolically, believing that somehow she would go directly into heaven without experiencing the physical pain of dying. In any case, she thanked the Lord for His mercy and lovingkindness and then she told the girls to do what was necessary to help her be a Christian martyr. She was ready for heaven and was looking forward with expectancy and joy to her martyrdom.

The girls went to great lengths preparing for this important ritual. They spread a red cloth on the floor, and Jeanne Marie knelt in the middle of it. They joined with her in a confession of faith in God the Father, Creator of heaven and earth, and in Jesus Christ the Son, crucified, risen and coming again in power and glory, and in the Blessed Holy Spirit at work in this world to convict sinners. It was a most impressive ritual. In all sincerity and with purity of heart the child did all the older girls required of her.

Then when Jeanne Marie was kneeling there in prayer with her rosary clutched tightly in her sweaty hands, one of the bigger girls raised a long sword high over her head. She stood poised—like she was about to bring it down. At that moment Jeanne Marie opened her tear-filled eyes and looked up at the sharp, shiny blade over her head. Suddenly realizing what was about to happen, she cried out, "Wait! Wait! You can't do this! It is not right that I should die without first getting my father's permission!"

The ritual ended abruptly.

The girls accused Jeanne Marie of stopping the proceedings at the last moment only to escape death. So far as they were concerned—and they told her so—her chance for martyrdom was past, lost forever, and she could go to hell and stay there. They said she would never be a Christian martyr now because she had offended God by not going through with her intention once the sacred process had been initiated.

Serious as she was about the whole thing, Jeanne Marie soon learned from the pointed jokes and stifled giggles that the older girls had used her wish to be a Christian martyr for their own entertainment. They had not meant one word that they said during the ritual.

This caused her to begin to doubt again. No matter what the Duchess, the nuns, the priest and her father did or said, Jeanne Marie felt depressed and convicted, certain she had offended the Blessed Lord and no longer sure whom she could trust.

This melancholy and despondence forced her to return home to the care of the servants after having spent two years in the Convent of the Benedictines. It was almost a year before she became a happy, trusting child again.

When Jeanne Marie had turned seven her father decided to place her in the Ursuline Seminary for a second time. Her two half-sisters were now teaching-nuns in this institution. Her father requested that she be under the supervision of his older daughter who, he felt, would provide a stable Christian example for Jeanne Marie to emulate. This proved to be a wise decision. The two were devoted to one another.

Because Jeanne Marie was so much younger than the other boarders, her association with the older girls was somewhat restricted while under the supervision of her half-sister. Besides regular scholastic studies, Jeanne Marie received guidance in Scripture reading, prayers and penances. She also learned how to conduct herself properly and to do the chores required of the girls in the convent.

Of course, her father enjoyed having Jeanne Marie at home as much as could be permitted without interfering with her education. One day he sent a message to the seminary for his eight-year-old daughter to come home. Jeanne Marie was always delighted when this happened. This time her father had a guest for her to meet. It was Queen Henrietta Maria of England and her traveling companions. He asked Jeanne Marie to entertain his distinguished guests. The Queen was so favorably impressed with the child's polite curtsies, her lively recitations, humorous responses and dances that she wanted the girl to accompany her to England to be the personal Maid of Honor to her daughter, the Princess.

Naturally, the girl was overjoyed at the prospect of trading the quietude of the seminary for the excitement of a trip to a foreign country. Were she to accompany Queen Henrietta Maria to England, she knew it would please her mother who was always looking for an opportunity to move into the halls of high-ranking society and social acceptance. How she wished her father would say "Yes" to the Queen's request.

Because of the political situation in England at this time, Queen Henrietta Maria, the daughter of King Henry IV and sister of King Louis XIII of France (father of Louis XIV now on the throne), was not occupying the throne of England. She had migrated to France in 1644, twelve years before, and was presently living in the Convent of Chaillet in abject poverty and without any visible means of support except donations from her political supporters. However, she tried to maintain the dignity worthy of her title. She kept in touch with the political situation in her homeland. She was perched ready to return to England when the time was right. There were many influential people on the European continent, as well as in England, who wanted to see her back in her own country.

But before the Queen's request could develop into anything more than a kind and thoughtful gesture toward Jeanne Marie, Monsieur de La Mothe thanked her and politely declined the invitation.

Jeanne Marie found herself back in the Ursuline Seminary, her dreams shattered. Besides this disappointment, she found upon her return to the seminary that her favorite half-sister had been assigned to other duties. Months later when Jeanne Marie came under the care of her half-sister again, her faith and devotion to God became more pronounced.

In the little convent garden chapel dedicated to the Christ Child, Jeanne Marie found a quiet place where she could meet God in solitude, away from the other girls and nuns. Here she went every morning for her private devotions. Taking her breakfast plate in hand, she would walk through the convent garden toward the little chapel like a soldier reporting for duty. No one questioned her actions, even though some of the nuns did observe her daily treks to and from the chapel. Of course the nuns were aware that this girl did resort to acts of devotion to show her love for Jesus. They knew she wanted so much to please the Lord Jesus. She loved to pray, sometimes spending hours on her knees with rosary and prayer book clutched in her hands. She frequently fasted more than was advisable for one so frail and young as she was.

Later, when the garden chapel was cleaned, her secret act of devotion was discovered and stopped immediately. There, behind the image of the Christ Child, were the uneaten remains of a goodly number of breakfasts. Apparently she had been hiding her food behind the image, depriving herself in the hope that God would accept it as her sacrifice to His dear Son. She wanted so much to be worthy of heaven. The nuns tried to explain to her as simply as possible how long fasting was not at all necessary or required of her, but Jeanne Marie had her own convictions and would not be moved.

• • • • •

"And Thou, O my God! didst leave me to myself, because I left Thee first, and wast pleased in permitting me to sink into the horrible pit, to make me feel the necessity of approaching Thee in soulful prayer.

"Thou didst leave me to myself, because I left Thee first. Yet such is Thy divine goodness that it seemed to me that Thou hadst left me with deep regret; and when this heart was desirous to return again unto Thee, with what speed didst Thou come to meet it. This proof of Thy love and mercy shall be to me an everlasting testimony of Thy goodness and of my own ingratitude."

—Madame Jeanne Guyon

3

Convent Schooling

Home now for a short time, Jeanne Marie Bouvieres de La Mothe had already spent some six years of her young life in convent boarding schools. Her previous stays in the family home at Montargis had been painfully brief, and this occasion was no exception. So no one, especially not ten-year-old Jeanne Marie, was surprised when, after a visit with the Prioress of the House of the Dominicans, her father smiled, patted her head and said, "Jeanne, my girl, I've decided to enroll you in the House of the Dominicans this season."

Jeanne Marie had always been in rather poor health, with recurring fever and weak spells periodically interrupting her formal schooling. Because of this and the fact that the House of the Dominicans was not a school catering to young children, her father questioned the Prioress as to the kind of care, attention, recreation and tutoring a ten-year-old would receive with the older, more physically and mentally mature girls.

"*Oui, oui*, Monsieur La Mothe. I will most assuredly look after your precious daughter very carefully. She will be like a child of my own. I shall devote my time to tutor Jeanne Marie myself. She's a most teach-able child. I shall see to her, monsieur. She will be with me every moment. Be assured. She will be ex-tremely well cared for."

At first this small religious community was a grand adventure for Jeanne Marie. Dressed in a child-sized nun's habit with her rosary and beads dangling freely from her neck, she would hurry along with the Prioress on her daily rounds throughout the convent and garden area, to choir and vespers, and in and out of the kitchen. Just as the Prioress had pledged, they were together almost constantly. The Prioress deeply adored the girl.

With the Prioress's tutoring, this intelligent child advanced rapidly in her studies. She attended reli-gious instruction classes with the other young lady boarders and took her turn in performing the easier everyday chores in the convent. She learned to sit, stand and walk in an acceptable manner, to show piety, to say her prayers and to practice the required virtues of Christian living. Then something occurred to alter the routine. Convent business demanded the Prioress's total attention, making it impossible for her to keep her promise to Monsieur de La Mothe any longer. Convent business had to come first.

Now, rather than have Jeanne Marie with the older girls too often, the Prioress was forced to leave the girl alone and unsupervised. She enjoyed the child's vibrant, happy spirit, and she missed the tu-toring sessions almost as much as Jeanne Marie did. But this was the way it had to be.

While sick with chicken pox, Jeanne Marie was

confined to her room for nearly three weeks. During this time she saw only the lay-sister who brought her tray of food and quickly departed. The other teaching-nuns and lay-sisters had enough to do without looking after a sick child, so they did not trouble themselves about her welfare. No one would come near for fear of contracting smallpox, which was the dread disease they supposed she had.

During this quarantine period Jeanne Marie began to reach out toward God once again. Avid reader that she was, the girl was delighted to find a Bible had been left in her room. How it happened, no one seemed to know. As a rule the girls in the convent school did not have access to the Bible other than during public readings at vespers. What a find! During the last two weeks of her quarantine she sometimes spent most of the day reading from the Bible, giving no attention to other books. Deeply absorbed in Bible reading, she memorized long Scripture portions. No doubt this early acquaintance with the Bible is what laid the foundation for and greatly influenced her later life of devotion and piety.

After about eight months in the House of the Dominicans, Jeanne Marie came home. Perhaps her father felt that his wife, who was good and charitable in many ways, would have more time for the girl now that Jeanne Marie was a little older and would not require so much care and training. Before long it was obvious that things were no different than before. Jeanne Marie had to get along the best she could. Her mother showed little interest in her. When it came to looking after the child, the servants did as they were ordered and little more. Sibling rivalry caused discord and disharmony in the home. Although Monsieur de La Mothe loved each child dearly, he had a special sympathy and understanding for his youngest daughter; but they saw little of each other except on weekends and holidays when he would be home. So it was that her father knew little, if anything, about the children's quarrels and the problems within the home.

Although Jeanne Marie loved her father, she also feared him and his volatile temper. So the less said, the better. She said nothing of the unfair treatment and difficulties facing her at home. It seemed as if everyone was against her —her mother, the servants, her younger brother. Even her older half-brother, when at home, would indulge himself in teasing and quarreling with her.

Jeanne Marie claimed that her mother favored the younger son over all the other children and gave the boy far more attention than anyone else. Jealousy, envy and strife grew in her heart as she tried, but failed, to cope successfully with her allegedly difficult role of family scapegoat. According to Jeanne Marie, her younger brother got by with all kinds of willful and deliberately mischievous behavior. Everyone generally gave in to his selfish demands. Whatever the boy did seemed to be condoned. This angered Jeanne Marie because she frequently was blamed for his mischief and the discord in the home.

When not quite twelve, Jeanne Marie expressed a desire to partake of the Sacrament of Holy Communion for the first time. Prior to this she honestly

tried at times to find God, but because of ambiva-
lent feelings about her spiritual need she became
rather remiss in the performance of her religious
duties. Consequently she concluded that religion, as
she had been taught it in convent schools, had not
benefited her any. Now she decided she would give
God another try. With renewed interest in the Roman Catholic Church she decided to take the next
step, in the hope of renewing her faith in the Lord
Jesus Christ. Holy Communion, she thought, was
the answer.

How pleased her father was to see this desire for
spiritual things manifest itself again in his favorite
daughter. That little flickering flame of faith was
still aglow in her heart. During the years in convent
schools Jeanne Marie had learned how to put on the
outward impression of a pious soul. Now, being aware
of the inner struggle between her good intentions
and her bad habits, Jeanne Marie thought most seriously about her spiritual needs. She spent hours reading the Bible, meditating and praying in an effort to
find the peace of God. Her father felt his older daughter, a teaching-nun in the Ursuline Seminary where
Jeanne Marie had previously spent three-and-a-half
years, could assist in preparing Jeanne Marie for this
act of religious devotion, her First Holy Communion. So he enrolled the girl there for the third time.

Under her half-sister's supervision she made many
desperate attempts to free her soul from sin and worldliness by prayer, fasting, going to confession and doing
penance. When Easter came she appeared to be well
prepared, and she received the Sacrament of Holy

Communion for the first time. How her soul yearned for the Blessed Savior to be ever by her side! Determined to show her love for God and the Lord Jesus Christ, she now desired more than anything else to know the will of God for the remainder of her life. The thought of giving herself wholly to God for His service entered into her thinking. At that moment she wanted more than anything else to become a nun. Such joy and spiritual elation as she had never before known flooded her receptive heart and soul.

Jeanne Marie left the seminary after Pentecost Sunday, only about seven weeks after Easter, an unhappy soul no better off spiritually than before she came. The spiritual joy that overwhelmed her at Easter simply had ebbed away. Those old habits, failures and shortcomings—including outbursts of temper, lying and quarreling—returned, snuffing out the spiritual joy she had experienced at her First Communion. How could this be? Had all her searching for God been in vain?

It does not matter to Satan if one is devoutly religious or not. Satan is clever in this respect. But he becomes enraged when a person surrenders himself wholly to the Lord's work. There is nothing Satan hates more than a Christian's determination to submit to God's will without reservation, like this girl had done at Easter when she took her First Communion.

Unfortunately Jeanne Marie began, at this critical period, to pursue a worldly path. In spite of all her religious training and association with nuns in her childhood, she had seemingly gained little of what could be termed real faith. Now the bright lights and excitement of the world, even in 1660, had much to offer an attractive young girl. Tall for her age and only twelve, Jeanne Marie was fast maturing into a beautiful, fascinating and complex woman. This pleased her mother no end. Madame de La Mothe at last was able to find satisfaction in her radiant daughter. Now she enjoyed dressing the girl in the most elegant and stylish clothes and showing her off at formal gatherings and social events. Jeanne Marie responded well to her mother's instructions on manners and behavior becoming a lady in the King's Court.

Because of the girl's beauty and vivacious charm, she was the center of attention at every party. Her witty conversation made her a favorite with everyone. As worldly interests and the gaudiness of high society beckoned strongly, her spiritual goals, religious duties and thoughts of God were soon laid aside.

Several eligible young men expressed their desire to marry her. However, her father would not approve of marriage at her young age. Then one day Monsieur De Toissi, a devout, young missionary cousin, stopped briefly in Montargis to visit his uncle's family while enroute to his assignment in Cochin China. Jeanne Marie happened to be out walking with friends and missed seeing him. Later, when told about his brief visit, she was greatly convicted by the Holy Spirit of God and overcome with remorse. Apparently the contrast between this cousin's dedication and her own worldliness revived in her a bit of that flickering flame of faith, reminding her of her backslidden condition. Conviction gripped her soul like a vice. Remembering how often she had heard God's call without obeying, she cried out in desperation and contriteness of heart.

She was later able to write, with reference to this time: "Oh, Thou God of love, how often hast Thou knocked at the door of my heart! Why didst Thou not, O my God, utterly take my heart to Thyself when I gave it to Thee so freely in my pure youthfulness? Or if Thou didst take it then, oh, why didst Thou let it revolt again? Thou wast surely strong enough to hold it; but Thou wouldst perhaps, in leaving me to myself, display Thy mercy that the depth of my iniquity might serve as a trophy of Thy goodness."

Early the next morning, while making her confession, she mused, "Father, am I the only person in our family to be lost? Alas! Help me in my desperate attempt at salvation. How sorry I am for having displeased God! What regrets I have! What tears of sorrow!"

Surprised at this emotional display of contrition, but not at all aware of her backslidden condition, the confessor-priest tenderly comforted her. In an effort to obtain forgiveness for every sin, she enumerated the small mistakes as well as the more obvious sins she had committed. Despite the fact that she failed to have complete assurance of her salvation at that time, a noticeable change did take place in her life. It was hard to believe she was the same person after an interval of only a couple weeks. She begged forgiveness of those whom she had knowingly wronged. She even apologized to the family servants. She determined never again to allow her own will to override what she knew to be the will of God.

The girl would shut herself away from all other activities to fast, pray, study the Bible and read devotional books. Saint Francis de Sales' writings, the *Life of Madame de Chantal*, and the still popular *Imitation of Christ* by Thomas à Kempis fascinated her and inspired her to even greater devotional heights. From these mystical religious writers she became conscious of the possibility of complete oneness with the Lord Jesus Christ.

In an attempt to receive the gift of spiritual prayer such as Madame Jane Frances de Chantal possessed, Jeanne Marie began to imitate the acts of piety mentioned in Madame de Chantal's writings. She read how this saintly woman branded the holy name of Jesus upon her person with a hot iron in an effort to follow literally, as she understood it, the Biblical admonition to "set the Lord's name as a seal upon your heart." Of course her parents would never approve of such a thing. But since she did admire Madame de Chantal so much, she felt she had to try to be like her. Unable to put aside this desire, she finally found a way to copy Madame de Chantal's act of piety. She wrote the word "Jesus" in large letters on pieces of paper. Then with needle and thread and some ribbon she sewed this name to her skin in four places, allowing it to remain there under her clothes in painful penance to the Lord.

This was only the beginning of a series of austerities Jeanne Marie inflicted upon herself in the years that followed. Attempting all the time to eradicate internal sin, she hoped to purge her body and soul from Satan's grasp. Wrong as it was, we have to remember that the Roman Catholic Church did advocate and encourage self-discipline of this nature among its adherents. Many of the very devout believed that in afflicting punishment upon their physical bodies they were making themselves more like their Blessed Savior and sharing in His suffering. A tender and sensitive person like Jeanne Marie Bouvieres de La Mothe naturally thought it right to emulate the devotional life of a saintly person she admired so much.

Claiming that Jesus Christ Himself had called her, Jeanne Marie decided to join the order of Saint Francis de Sales to become a nun. When Jeanne Marie asked for her father's permission to enter this nunnery, his loud and immediate "No!" came as no real surprise. Although encouraged by her renewed interest in the Church, he was far from convinced that the restrictive life of a nun was for his pretty daughter. He was of the opinion that God's will could be done in the secular world much better than behind the walls of a cloistered nunnery, aloof from the daily existence of the present world.

But Jeanne Marie was not one to give up easily.

Since her father was frequently away on business, she thought she could enter the nearby Convent of Saint Francis de Sales without him knowing it. Then when he returned home and found out, it would be too late for him to withdraw her. Knowing full well that her mother shared her father's opinion in this matter, Jeanne Marie saw no reason to seek her mother's consent. One night she took matters into her own hands and went to the convent, begging the nuns to accept her. Realizing this would only lead to trouble for all concerned, the nuns did not dare to admit her without her father's written permission. But to pacify the child, they granted her the privilege of visiting her cousin who resided there. So she did not become a nun after all.

After another year of earnestly seeking God, Jeanne Marie's attention turned to other things. She fell in love with a devoutly religious young man. They wanted to marry, but there was one problem: they were cousins. Therefore her father refused to give his consent, not so much because the girl was only fourteen years of age but because of the difficulty involved in obtaining sanction from the Pope for a marriage of two close blood relations.

Dissatisfied with the way things turned out, Jeanne Marie felt utterly frustrated and alone in the world. From events in later years we must assume that this young man had been Jeanne Marie's one true love. After their acquaintance and courtship came to an end, she tried to forget him. It is doubtful that she ever completely convalesced from the hurt of this broken engagement. Outwardly she kept up a strictly religious appearance, doing what was expected of a devout Roman Catholic. She prayed faithfully to the saints and to the Blessed Virgin Mary, Mother of Jesus, for the forgiveness of sins and the preservation of her soul from the torment of hell, went to confession often, and took Holy Communion every two weeks at the nearby parish church. Even though she was going through the motions of a religious life, she knew her true standing was that of a backslidden soul. To cover the hurt in her heart she began reading romantic novels and spent hours vainly admiring herself in the mirror. But nothing, absolutely nothing, could fill the emptiness, no matter what activity she directed herself to.

From time to time the Holy Spirit reminded her of God's love. Then she remembered the joy of salvation she once knew. She longed to be restored to a right relationship with the Lord and Savior Jesus Christ whom she once loved so deeply. This gave her the courage to sail over the tumultuous events soon to occur in her life.

· · · · ·

"How I rejoice to owe all to Thee. And that Thou favorest my heart with a sight of the treasures and boundless riches of Thy grace and love! Thou hast dealt with me as if a magnificent king should marry a poor slave—forget her slavery, give her all the ornaments which may render her completely pleasing to his eyes like a sunrise on a clear warm day, and freely pardon all the faults and ill qualities which her ignorance and bad education has given her. This Thou hast made my case. My poverty is become my riches. And in the extremity of my weakness I have found my strength. I made verses and little songs to bewail myself. I exercised austerities, but they did not satisfy my heart. They were like those drops of water which only serve to make the fire hotter.

"When I take a view of God and of myself, I am obliged to cry out, 'Oh, admirable conduct of Love toward an ungrateful wretch! Oh, horrible ingratitude toward such unparalleled goodness'"

—Madame Jeanne Guyon

4

Courtship and Marriage

All of France felt the effect of King Louis XIV's absolute monarchy in the seventeenth century. In fact, this period in French history, called the "century of Louis XIV," saw his seventy-two-year reign (1643-1715) as the longest in modern European history. It was without a doubt the most pleasure-loving, corrupt and dissolute as well as the most expensive and extravagant rule of any king in all of France's long existence. He almost bankrupted the nation with all his extravagance and worldliness.

Louis XIV had succeeded his father, Louis XIII, to the throne when he was a mere lad of four. His mother, Anna of Austria, acted as regent until 1661, the year the scheming prime minister Cardinal Mazarin died. King Louis XIV, then about twenty-two years of age, proclaimed himself to be his own prime minister and proudly bragged, "*L'etat c'est moi*" — "I am the State." He is referred to as Louis the Great because he is the prime example of an absolute monarch. This man had two all-consuming desires—to make France great, and to make himself the prime source of his country's greatness. Every action on his part was geared toward these goals.

Where there is a king there usually is a queen. In this case it was Marie Therese of Spain, whom Louis XIV married in 1660. But his several mistresses, especially Madame de Maintenon, appealed to him more than his wife ever could. In reality, Madame de Maintenon—to whom King Louis XIV was secretly married after the Queen's death—was always the ruling power behind the throne.

To increase the pomp and ceremony surrounding the majesty of the throne, the King assigned jobs to the most skilled, influential and prominent people, thus employing for his own use the most talented and prosperous craftspeople in the entire kingdom. Monuments and public works were turned into magnificent structures that would laud his personal ambition and acclaim his appreciation for the arts, literature and French culture for centuries yet to come. No expense was spared in constructing the royal palace in Versailles, which was to be both the King's residence and the location of the King's Court. Nobles, dukes, and ladies of high rank and royalty resided there in grandeur never before seen on this earth. In fact, so many nobles and dukes lived at the royal palace that France became a nation of absentee landlords who maintained little or no contact with their tenants. The extravagance of King Louis XIV's court life compounded France's already vast financial problems, and ironically, also hid this dangerous situation behind the facade King Louis XIV had erected at such an expense.

In 1663, when the Claude Bouvieres de La Mothe family moved from Montargis to Paris, Paris was also the center of scientific and literary achievement of the seventeenth century. With its wondrous sights, affluence, high society and fashionable amusements, Paris was a fast-moving, worldly, pleasure-seeking city. All of this extravagance, seeming superiority, voluptuousness and social activity pleased Madame de La Mothe, who did everything within her power to make her beautiful teen-age daughter Jeanne Marie accepted in these fashionable circles. Perhaps Monsieur de La Mothe's position and rank was itself the reason they came to the capital city. If so, this explains their becoming so involved in King Louis XIV's Court.

Like a graceful Grecian model, well-built and somewhat tall for her age, fifteen-year-old Jeanne Marie with her sparkling clear eyes, broad forehead, fair complexion, dark hair and round face was indeed a classic French beauty. Everything in Paris appealed to her vanity and heightened her personal pride. The arts, culture, refinement, fashions and amusements of every description were there for the younger generation to enjoy to the fullest. As a child Jeanne Marie had been inclined toward Christian ways. Now, as an impressionable young lady, she became a vain, proud social butterfly carried away by the excitement of her big city surroundings. Jeanne Marie was extremely susceptible to the influence of such elegant society, having already made her debut. She possessed real charm, intellect and poise. Her ability to engage in interesting conversation, as well as her outstanding beauty, demanded her presence at every party and social event in Paris and at the royal palace in Versailles.

Several youthful suitors eagerly approached her father for permission to marry his beautiful daughter. But he refused them all. None of their proposals were quite acceptable enough. Perhaps due to the family's strained financial status, he wanted to be certain his daughter would marry none but the most affluent and eligible man available.

It would appear that money did become the deciding factor in his decision because of the marriage arrangement he later made for Jeanne Marie with Monsieur Jacques Guyon, a successful, wealthy, thirty-eight-year-old man from a most distinguished French family.

Jacque's father and a Monsieur Bouterour had engineered and completed construction of the Canal of Briare, which connects the River Loire with the Seine. This was the very first such project ever undertaken in France. It had been a long time from start to finish, but at the completion of this tremendous project the French government paid these men a handsome sum. With this money the older Jacques Guyon made some good investments and soon became a wealthy man. Cardinal Richelieu, who was prime minister then, awarded Monsieur Guyon a patent of nobility in appreciation for the great help he had been to the government in building this canal. It was this noble title of Seigneur (Lord) de Chesney that was later passed down to his son.

Family-arranged marriages were the usual custom of that day. So after conferring a number of times with Jacques Guyon, Jeanne Marie's parents accepted his offer. Then on January 28, 1664, they had her sign the Articles of Marriage without telling her the true nature of the document she hastily signed just to please them.

Like most young girls, Jeanne Marie looked forward to marriage; that is, after she gave up the idea of becoming a nun. She dreamed of a happy-ever-after sort of togetherness with her prince charming on his sleek white charger, taking her away from all the problems and drudgery she'd ever known. To most young women, Monsieur Jacques Guyon would have been that prince charming. But to Jeanne Marie, who was to be given in marriage to this man, Monsieur Jacques Guyon was not the man she would have preferred to marry at all. He was much too old. He was not even good-looking. Worst of all, there was no love between them. So what did it matter that he had inherited money, properties, and a business with an annual income of forty thousand livres—plus a noble position in French society? Jeanne Marie did not love Jacques. But the marriage contract had been signed and there was no way she could break it.

About to be married to a man she did not love, Jeanne Marie prayed with a most sincere and contrite attitude, "Oh, my God, how great is Thy goodness to bear with me at this time, and to allow me to pray to Thee with as much boldness as if I were one of Thy friends. I, who have rebelled against Thee as Thy greatest enemy." In an attempt to know where God's will fit into her forthcoming marriage, she had masses said and candles lit at the altar in her behalf. All the while, of course, she was aware that there was no alternative. She had to go through with the marriage in accordance with the parental agreement made with Monsieur Jacques Guyon, since this paper carried the weight of a legal document.

Three days before the wedding date the couple were introduced to each other. Then on March 21, 1664, Jeanne Marie, not quite sixteen years old, and Jacques Guyon, twenty-two years older than his bride, were united in holy matrimony. Amid all the wild rejoicing and pompous congratulating that followed this very fashionable wedding ceremony, the new bride nearly collapsed in what could be described as a state of shock. Her heart was heavy, laden down with sadness, disappointment and despair. Its every beat reminded her that love had absolutely no part in this union. She had simply entered into this marriage out of respect for her father's judgment in choosing a proper mate for her.

Recalling her earlier desire to give herself to God, Jeanne Marie, now the young and beautiful Madame Guyon, cried bitter tears on her wedding day. "Alas! I had desired to be a nun; why then am I now married to such a worldly creature, and for such a mundane purpose too?"

The home to which her husband brought her turned out to be a far cry from that happy-ever-after dream of her girlhood fantasies. In many ways her marriage, husband, and position in the home proved to be a trial from the first moment she crossed the Guyon threshold. Now as the wife of the wealthy Monsieur Jacques Guyon, a man old enough to be her father, she came to appreciate her own family's relatively tranquil household. Perhaps things had not been as bad as she had thought after all. Jeanne Marie had to admit that in spite of the way her mother and the other children had mistreated her, she had been raised well in elegance and generosity and had come to genuinely appreciate beauty and culture.

Her husband's widowed and wizened mother, a morally good but jealously possessive woman when it came to her son, continued to live in and rule the house and the domestic servants as if it all belonged to her. The older Madame Guyon refused to recognize her son's young bride as the woman of the house. To her, nothing was as important as money. She guarded every centime as if it were the last to be had, seeing to it that every coin was accounted for and nothing wasted. Since young Jeanne Marie had never concerned herself about food, shelter, clothes and other home necessities before, it was perhaps just as well that her mother-in-law took responsibility for these things.

With her husband totally possessed and domineered by his mother, it did Jeanne Marie no good to complain about the situation. She just had to learn to cope with it, no matter how difficult and degrading it was.

Both Jacques' mother and the servants gave Jeanne Marie a hard time. They intimidated her by scolding and criticizing all she did, ridiculing her family and, in general, making her the object of their jest. At first this happened mostly when Monsieur Guyon was absent. But before long even he, pressured by his mother, frowned upon Jeanne Marie's efforts to please him. He allowed her little opportunity to express her own feelings and opinions within the family circle. Life became a torturous existence for her.

On many occasions young Madame Guyon found herself in a world in which she seemed not to belong. Later, in her autobiography, she referred to herself as "a child of another world"—as being one alone with God. She described her frustration: "Married to a person of rank and wealth, I found myself a slave in my own dwelling, rather than the free person I had imagined and expected myself to become." But distasteful as her marriage was, there could be no getting out of it. As circumstances within the Guyon household proved to be most intolerable to her, she withdrew into herself more and more. It was during these times of aloneness that she began to see her need for God's assurance and comfort. This recognition, along with growing reliance upon the Lord Jesus for inner strength and stability, brought peace and intense joy to her soul once again.

United in marriage with this man "for better or for worse, for richer or for poorer, in sickness and in health, until death . . . ," Jeanne Marie came to respect Jacques for his personal kindness toward her when they were alone together.

After four months of marriage it was learned that Jacques suffered from gout, an ailment that sometimes put him in bed for five or six weeks and otherwise necessitated his use of a crutch or walking stick. For this reason a nursemaid was hired to assist him constantly.

Just before the birth of their first son, Armand Jacques Guyon, in 1665, nearly a year after their marriage, the young Madame Guyon became ill. It was feared that she would die leaving no heir to the Guyon family fortune. To prevent this tragedy, her mother-in-law was obliged to give her pregnant daughter-in-law the most careful and considerate attention she could possibly manage. Needless to say, there was great rejoicing in the Guyon household over the successful delivery of a baby boy.

This child brought into Madame Guyon's life a new sense of happiness and purpose, which she shared with her husband. She was truly happy with this added family responsibility. She also remained faithful to her Lord, whom she credited with the strength she found to survive her pregnancy. Perhaps her life was to become a more happy one now—only time would tell.

. . . . .

By suffering only can we know
   The true nature of the life we live;
The trials of our souls, they show,
   How true, how pure, the love we give.
To leave my love in doubt would be
No less disgrace than utter misery.

I welcome, then, with open heart sincere,
   The cross My Savior bids me take;
No load, no trial is too severe,
   That's borne or suffered for His divine sake.
And thus my sorrows shall proclaim
A love that's worthy of the name.

          —Madame Jeanne Guyon

5

Trying Times

Unfortunately, things were not always pleasant for the young Madame Guyon in the proceeding years. Her husband's bad investments brought disastrous financial losses to the family. Actually, this did not change their lives to any great extent, and at a later date he managed to recoup most of his losses. But his mother was affected the most. She blamed Jeanne Marie for all the problems that came to the family and attributed Jacques' business reverses to his young wife, even though Jeanne Marie was not a party to them.

"No afflictions befell us till you came into this house," she lamented. "All these misfortunes came with you. You are a curse upon this house."

Then came the news of Madame Guyon's half-sister's death at the Ursuline Seminary. It came as a great disappointment and shock, but Jeanne Marie remembered this nun's prayers and teaching. Right away she set about in a concerted effort to change her ways, feeling convicted by the Holy Spirit because of her own worldliness. This half-sister's influence upon her had been good and it had lasting effects.

Desiring to set her life in order, Madame Guyon embarked on a personal reform program. To further examine herself and judge whether she was actually reforming, she kept a journal such as was required of persons in religious vocations. In it she recorded her faults in minute detail week by week. She also decided to put up her hair in a rather plain style. She stopped using make-up and paid less attention to her appearance. Now she rarely viewed herself in the mirror but left it up to the maidservant to select her clothes and comb her hair. While the maidservant helped her dress, Madame Guyon would read devotional books aloud so that anyone in the house who happened to be nearby might benefit from the reading.

During this trying time when Madame Guyon was seeking to renew her relationship with God, a number of Christians helped in guiding her toward the straight and narrow way that leads to life everlasting—a pious lady, her own missionary cousin, and a young Franciscan monk. Nor were they the only instruments God used.

The pious lady had rented one of her father's apartments. One day in conversing with Madame Guyon, who was back home for a visit, she made the simple remark that Madame Guyon had not yet attained the right attitude for mental prayer, and that she needed this in order to experience an honest inward relationship to God. This lady showed Christ's love and the presence of God's Holy Spirit in all that she did. Madame Guyon wanted so much to attain this same peaceful, Christlike attitude. She tried to emulate her by concentrating on devotional meditations, Bible study and long periods of prayer. Finally, the truth dawned upon her: something more enduring was needed. Try as she might, she could not put upon herself the likeness of Christ.

When her missionary cousin, Monsieur de Toissi, returned some months later from the Far East, Madame Guyon was overjoyed to see him. She knew she could be frank in talking with him about the spiritual matters that so disturbed her. Four years prior to this, his visit to her father's house had affected her greatly even though she did not have the opportunity to see him. Now, upon meeting the pious lady in the La Mothe apartment, Monsieur de Toissi agreed to help all he could while in Paris and joined with her in praying for Jeanne Marie's salvation.

Time passed. Then one day, as if by God's divine providence, a devout young Franciscan monk happened upon the La Mothe home. He felt the Lord Jesus Christ had directed his steps there, perhaps so that he might lead an influential man to know the Savior. Instead, he was introduced to Madame Guyon, pregnant at this time with her second child. She had come home due to her father's grave illness. Certainly their meeting must have been directed by the Lord—to "coincidentally" have Madame Guyon at her father's house when this monk arrived.

Of course, principles of the Christian faith dominated their conversation. This monk impressed Madame Guyon as being a true Christian. Later, when she wanted to consult him on spiritual matters, she took another woman along for appearance's sake and talked with him privately while her companion waited. How she hungered to know God! How she searched to find Him! She confessed to this monk how she had given herself to prayer, Bible reading, church attendance and charitable works, but had not found that spiritual joy she had once known. She even confided in him about the penances and general confession she had recently made.

"Your efforts have heen unsuccessful, madame, because you have sought externally what you can only find within your soul. Accustom yourself to seek God in your heart, and you will not fail to find Him." He said she should be encouraged in her search for the reality of God, and advised her to seek her soul's salvation through simple faith in Jesus Christ, crucified and risen again, not by outward good works—as she had been attempting so vainly.

At that moment something remarkable happened to her. She felt uplifted . . . like a cloud quietly drifting high above the hustling city. Immediately she knew that somehow God had touched her soul and changed her heart. Such unction, joy and spiritual freedom! She could not find words to tell how elated she felt. Then she realized that at last she had found the precious Lord Jesus and allowed Him to be her own Savior. She couldn't sleep that night. Later she wrote of this in her autobiography: "Thy love, O my God, flowed in me like a delicious oil, and burned as fire which was going to devour all that was left of self."

From then on her life took on a vitally new perspective. It was on Saint Magdalen's Day, July 22,

1668, that the angels in heaven rejoiced over this sinner that had come so humbly home! A new name was recorded in Glory: Madame Jeanne Marie Bouvieres de La Mothe Guyon!

From the day of her conversion Madame Guyon resolved: "If it be possible, I will be wholly the Lord's. The world shall have no portion in me whatsoever." Some months later she told the Franciscan monk, "I love God far more than the most affectionate lover among men loves the object of his earthly attachment." What the pious lady, Jeanne Marie's missionary cousin and this Franciscan monk tried to show her was possible finally had become a reality! Twenty years old and truly born again by the power of the living God, Madame Guyon was now at peace with God! Cleansed from sin! Happy in the Lord!

What a dramatic change came to this once so active social butterfly! The change in her was unmistakably wrought by the operation of the Holy Spirit. Her understanding of spiritual things was enlightened. With no dreams, no visitation, nothing audible, that "still, small voice" spoke loudly to her soul, guiding her past the temptations of the world. To be wholly the Lord's wasn't easy in the hostile environment of the Guyon household. It would have been difficult even for a saint to maintain a constant Christian witness there. Madame Guyon was certainly no saint by birth. Now, however, because life was not very pleasurable to her in this world, except as her life was hidden in Christ, Madame Guyon called herself "a child of another world."

Passage from the natural, mundane life to that

resulting from spiritual rebirth differs with various people. For Madame Guyon the transition was slowly progressive in its preparatory steps, decisive and marked at the time it actually happened. So altered was she from her old self that she hardly recognized herself now that she was converted and born again by the Spirit of God. Pride and sullenness melted away into humility and praise as Madame Guyon became willing to look to the Lord Jesus alone as her hope and assurance of eternal salvation.

Some of her family and friends did not understand what had happened. She had suddenly said goodbye to worldly amusements and such pastimes as plays, dances and parties, denouncing all that money, nobility and the city of Paris had to offer for the austerity of her new path. She tried to conform to what she understood to be the Holy Spirit's wishes in modesty of dress, way of life, mental attitude, personal habits, disposition and conversation. To her, the Blessed Savior was so real, the Holy Bible so precious, the Holy Spirit so close! When adverse circumstances and things became hard for her, Madame Guyon tried to keep a sweet spirit about her continually. To refrain from saying something she might regret, she would shut her eyes, withdraw herself from the situation, and force herself to recall portions of Scripture and to praise God silently in her trembling heart.

In the background there was always her gossiping mother-in-law stirring up trouble. Worse than this was the fact that her husband habitually turned for guidance and advice to his mother instead of to his wife. Although Madame Guyon never claimed to love this man, she did respect and admire him as her lawful husband and freely admitted his many good qualities. He was an exceptionally intelligent man of good character and a prominent, respected businessman in his community. But being married to him was always such a burden to Jeanne Marie.

Apparently, at times Jacques Guyon did show genuine affection for Jeanne Marie. But try as she would to be a dutiful wife and a good mother, how could she be happy with a husband for whom she had no true love? Never could the Guyon wealth and noble rank in French society compensate for the difference in their ages, his physical ailments, his haughty ways, quick temper, and the constant interference from his aged mother.

Late in 1668 a second son was born to them, and the following year a daughter. With these three children, Madame Guyon's time was taken up with their care and doing what was necessary in the home. Five children in all were born to her and Jacques Guyon during their twelve years and four months of marriage.

For about two years after her conversion Madame Guyon lived on a spiritual mountaintop, rejoicing in the Lord regardless of how she was treated on the corporeal plane by others. The petty ridicule and mistreatment from her mother-in-law and the household servants was not easy to accept. But she was learning to cope with it. Then her own mother died, leaving her with no one to whom she could take her troubles except the Lord. To offset the loss of her mother she would accompany her husband on business trips to Orleans or Touraine more often now. What grief filled her soul when she realized that she was not exempt from temptation. The old life, she discovered, was still appealing and exciting.

Fearful now of backsliding, she looked for someone to instruct her on how to maintain a closer walk with the Lord and how to live a victorious Christian life. So upon returning home she went immediately to her dear friend and spiritual counselor Sister Genevieve Granger, the Prioress at the House of the Benedictines. To help Madame Guyon understand more fully how she could dedicate her whole existence to the Lord, Sister Granger recommended the recognized mystic Monsieur Bertot as her spiritual director. She hoped this godly man could help. But for some reason Madame Guyon found it most difficult, almost impossible in fact, to relate her problems to him. Most of their consultations turned out to be nothing but painfully long periods of silence.

On a typical dreary day in Paris, enroute to the famous Notre Dame Cathedral to pray, Madame Guyon was met by a young priest. Although a stranger, he seemed to know her. He commented to her about the things of God.

"My dear lady," he said, "God requires not merely a forgiven heart, but a holy heart as well. Surely you do realize it isn't enough to escape hell. God wants more than that from you. God demands the subjection of one's own nature and wants utmost purity of heart so you can reach the heights of Christian attainment."

Feeling the witness of God's Holy Spirit to what this priest told her, Madame Guyon entered Notre Dame Cathedral and fainted away. Awed by what had happened, she knew God's call was upon her life. She went home more determined than ever to make whatever sacrifice was necessary to yield herself completely to God's will. By now she had learned, when facing temptation, how much she needed to know God's Word and how dependent she had to be upon the Lord's sustaining strength and power daily.

"I became deeply assured of what the prophet said," she wrote in her autobiography. "Except the Lord keep the city, the watchman waketh but in vain. When I looked directly to Thee, O my Lord, Thou wast my Faithful Keeper; Thou didst continually defend my heart against all kinds of enemies. But alas!—when left to myself I was all weakness, like an amoeba changing in relation to my neighbors to better fit in with them. How easily did my enemies prevail over me!"

In the fall of 1670 a siege of illness hit the whole family. First her husband was confined to his bed with the gout again. Then their little daughter and oldest son were stricken with smallpox. Finally Madame Guyon took sick also. In her autobiography she recorded in detail the progress of this dread disease. During the last days of her illness she praised God silently as she lay in bed so weak, thinking she was about to die. When she resigned herself to dying and returning to her Creator, unspeakable joy filled her soul.

Since she strongly believed there was a purpose

in all things, she was convinced God had allowed her beauty to be permanently marred by smallpox scars in order to make her more humble. Therefore she made absolutely no effort to restore her facial appearance, accepting the pockmarks as another manifestation of the Lord's overwhelming presence.

The real blow came when their second son, whom both she and her husband loved dearly, died in the agonies of smallpox. He was but two years of age. Jacques Guyon grieved much over his son's death, but Madame Guyon accepted it as the will of God, saying, "The Lord gave and the Lord has taken away. Blessed be His holy name forever!"

In July 1671, Father Francois La Combe, an eminent Superior of the Barnabite order, came to the Guyon household with a letter of introduction from Father La Mothe, Madame Guyon's half brother. After this initial visit both looked forward to another meeting—Madame Guyon, to obtain spiritual guidance; Father La Combe, because he was impressed by this woman's Biblical knowledge and deep inward presence and awareness of God. Father La Combe soon became spiritual director to the Guyon household, at her request, taking the opportunity to visit frequently both husband and wife. He remained a close personal friend for many years.

Although Monsieur Guyon now allowed his wife to contribute toward charitable works without humiliating questioning, he continued to ridicule her for her "fanatic" religious practices. He sometimes limited her church attendance and withheld her Bible reading privileges at home. When he discovered that these measures failed in changing his wife's ways, he became irritable, angry and jealous.

"What! You love God so much that you would love me no longer!" he shouted, throwing his crutch across the room.

Whether he knew it or not, Monsieur Guyon's accusation was true. Since their marriage had never been based on mutual love, a kind of superficial affection passed between them merely as a marital duty acknowledged to the other. Her soul's highest aspiration was to reach up in faith to worship God in spirit and in truth. In a sense, you might say that even then Madame Guyon was already married to her Blessed Lord and Savior.

Knowing that Madame Guyon always commemorated the date of her conversion, July 22, Sister Genevieve Granger wrote suggesting that she add to her act of consecration and commemorate this fourth anniversary of her conversion in a very special way—by signing a marriage covenant with the Savior. This solemn form of mystical espousal with the Lord Jesus Christ was based upon the Holy Scriptures which speak of the true Church as the Bride of Christ. "The marriage of the Lamb is come, and His wife hath made herself ready. And to her was granted that she should be arrayed in fine linen, clean and white: for the fine linen is the righteousness of saints"—Revelation 19:7–8. This document was similar to the *Act of the Covenant* or the *Act of Consecration* which cloistered nuns signed at their final profession of faith. Upon this altar of sacrifice—Sister Genevieve pointed out—her will, natural desires, and

sincerity of devotion to the Lord could express themselves as in the Apostle Paul's prayer: "Lord, what
wilt Thou have me to do?"

This suggested marriage covenant with Jesus, her
Blessed Lord and Savior, made her poignantly conscious of His abiding presence in a more positive
and personal way than was previously imaginable.
So with joybells of gladness ringing in her heart and
soul, she affixed the signature *Madame Jeanne M. B.
de La Mothe Guyon* to the document. It read in part
as follows: "I henceforth take Jesus Christ to be mine.
I promise to receive Him as a husband to me. And I
give myself to Him, unworthy though I am, to be
His spouse. I ask of Him, in this marriage of spirit
with Spirit, that I may be of the same mind with
Him—meek, pure, nothing in myself, and united to
God's will. And, pledged as I am to be His, I accept,
as a part of my marriage portion, the temptations
and sorrows, the crosses and the contempt which
fell to Him."

· · · · ·

My heart is easy, and my burden light;
I smile, though sad, when God is in my sight.
The more my woes in secret I deplore,
I taste Thy goodness, and I love Thee more.

There, while a solemn stillness reigns around,
Faith, love, and hope within my soul abound;
And while the world suppose me lost in care,
The joys of angels unperceived I share.

Thy creatures wrong Thee, O Thou Sovereign God!
Thou art not loved, because not understood,
This grieves me most, that vain pursuits beguile
Ungrateful men, regardless of Thy smile.

Frail beauty and false honor are adored;
While Thee they scorn, and trifle with Thy Word;
Pass, unconcern'd, a Savior's sorrows by,
And hunt their ruin with a zeal to die.

—Madame Jeanne Guyon

6

Problems and
Widowhood at Twenty-eight

A distinctly peculiar thing, which Madame Guyon often referred to as her "state of privation" or "desolation of the soul," began in 1674 and continued to plague her tremendously for about six years. It came upon her even though all that had happened thus far to her family she had managed to accept without question. In July 1672, her father died. Although she had a premonition of his death, she arrived home too late for the burial. That same month their little three-year-old daughter died from a cerebral hemorrhage. She took this loss as stoically as she had the death of their second son: it was the will of God. But when her friend and spiritual counselor Sister Genevieve Granger died a few months later, she was deeply affected. Now with both her parents and Sister Granger gone, there was no one for her to lean upon in time of perplexity.

At times she would drop from the high mountaintop of spiritual ecstasy into a deep, depressive spiritual emptiness, totally lacking that joy and inner peace that had characterized her former Christian life. There seemed to be a desperate void in her personal relationship with the Lord. Where previously she had found happiness and personal satisfaction in serving God and ministering to others in the name of Jesus, now she went about doing good without feeling God's presence and blessing upon her efforts. She was like a person adrift in a lifeboat, lost on the high seas with nary a map or a single star's light for guidance.

To survive this bewildering experience of desolation Madame Guyon secured her husband's permission to spend several days at Saint Cyr's Convent in a spiritual retreat to receive help from a Sister Garnier who seemed to understand her current problem.

At Saint Cyr's Convent the methodical practice of mortification—the use of instruments of penance—was commonplace and shared by all. In those days the devout believed penances of this nature enabled the human soul to attain a closer relationship to God. It was thought to be a means for obtaining forgiveness of sins, spiritual strength, and special favors from God. Instruments of penance were used in convents and seminaries by those persons desiring to purify their souls, to attain a life of holiness, and thus make themselves worthy to be followers of Christ.

Trying to cut off all distracting contact with the world, Madame Guyon exposed herself to all types of physical deprivations and austerities. She wanted desperately to obtain absolution for her sins and to give herself wholly to God. She would fast for unbearably long periods, taking only small quantities of juice into her system. She scourged herself across the shoulders, arms and legs with knotted cords until blood came to the surface. She even resorted to wearing a broad belt of horsehair and nettles braided together, a girdle set with sharp nails poking into her bare flesh, and knee and elbow bracelets studded with blunt chunks of metal. But try as she did, there was absolutely nothing spiritual gained by such self-discipline. She left Saint Cyr's disappointed.

Where was the joy she had once known? Could it be that she was no longer a Christian? Had God forsaken her? Why was it, she reasoned to herself, that her salvation wavered so—up and down, up and down? Was not Jesus Christ's grace sufficient to save the soul once and for all?

Even though this woman's first love was her Heavenly Bridegroom, the Lord Jesus Christ, she remained a true and faithful wife to Jacques Guyon. During his lingering illness she cared for him with real tenderness and sympathy. Loyal always to him, she hardly left his bedside the last three-and-a-half weeks of his ordeal. Once when they were alone, she knelt beside his bed begging forgiveness for anything she might have done that had displeased him during their marriage.

To this he replied, "No! No! It is I who humbly beg your pardon. I did not ever deserve one as saintly as you."

So Monsieur Guyon finally came to appreciate his wife, preferring now to have her attend him instead of his elderly mother or the nursemaid. Because of this reconciliation they discovered a closeness previously missing in their relationship. However, there were occasions yet when Jacques was still quick tempered and unreasonable in his demands.

At times when his discomfort and suffering increased, he prayed to God for death to come. After receiving the last rites of the Roman Catholic Church, the Sacraments of Holy Communion and Extreme Unction, with heartfelt repentance and humility of spirit, he dropped into a deep coma from which he never recovered. He died on the morning of July 21, 1676, leaving his bereaved twenty-eight-year-old widow Jeanne Marie, their two sons, ages eleven and three, and an infant daughter born only a few weeks prior to his death. They were well provided for financially, however.

When advised of her husband's death, Madame Guyon was unable to cry—unable to utter a word, for that matter. Whatever it was that affected her so deeply, it could not have been the shock of his dying, as she was expecting this for many weeks. The next day she closed herself in her room and knelt in prayer with a rosary clutched in her hand. There, before an image of her Heavenly Bridegroom, the Lord Jesus Christ, she renewed her marriage covenant to Jesus, adding to it a vow of chastity—with the resolved intention to make her chastity perpetual should her spiritual director permit. Such radiantly euphoric joy came into her soul at that moment as she had never before experienced. She thought she could see hovering angels smiling their approval from the clouds in the bright blue sky overhead.

"Oh, my God, truly I am Thy servant," she cried out. "Thou hast broken my bonds, and I will offer Thee a sacrifice of thanksgiving, and will call upon the name of the Lord."

True to her commitment, she regarded herself as belonging entirely to Christ. Now she recognized that the time had come to devote her life exclusively to His work. But being left a rich young widow, only twenty-eight years old, did not free her immediately to follow the Lord, no matter how certain she was of His call. Besides the three children, her mother-in-law and the servants, she was now responsible for the family business and her late husband's estate, all of which had to be dealt with first.

The administration of her late husband's estate proved to be a very difficult task, involving a complicated inventory. Many debtors and creditors had to be approached. To complete contracts, assessment sheets, business interests and legacies, many legal papers and briefs had to be filed. All this took time and work far beyond what she thought would be necessary. She knew little about his architectural business and had cared even less. Now it was hers to sift through, inexperienced as she was. But she soon found a way to solve these weighty problems. First, she prayed about the matter. Then she consulted her legal advisor. And—yes, things did work out! Persons acquainted with the nature of Monsieur Guyon's work marveled at how efficiently his widow handled the situation. Some things that had been long pending she was able, with the Lord's help, to settle, satisfying all concerned.

Things were far from easy, though. Arrangements had to be made to care for her elderly mother-in-law during her remaining years. Legacies were to go to various relatives as well as generous annuities to the household servants in recognition of their faithful service. Although her late husband's nursemaid had been well paid and dismissed, this woman preferred to stay on to help with the children, continuing to be a source of irritation to Madame Guyon. Every attempt at reconciliation with her mother-in-law failed miserably. For the past twelve years they had always been at odds with one another. Now that these two women were left to look after the children and family affairs together, their relationship was limited to simply tolerating each other's presence under the same roof with a coolness bordering on frigidity.

During the winter of 1676-77, about six months after her husband's death, Madame Guyon took her three children and moved from the family mansion to a residence of their own. For a while she tried to live in seclusion, leaving the house only to attend Mass and confession and, occasionally, to go marketing. Her concern was to find the will of God for her life by becoming a knowledgeable student of the Bible. Already an avid reader of the Bible, she felt compelled to study approved Roman Catholic books that would help her understand the Holy Scripture. Since most religious books at that time were written in Latin, Madame Guyon took up home study of this language. This was a difficult thing for a woman to do in those days. Every night after studying by candlelight she would retire late, with red, bleary eyes, and awaken the next morning to resume her regimen that included care of the children, household chores, sewing and gardening.

Amid all this she prayed earnestly, "Lord, what would you have me to do?"

It seemed that an inner voice kept calling out in anguish and in pain: "Geneva ... Geneva ... Geneva!"

What can this possibly mean? she wondered in her most lucid moments. The mere thought of Geneva was shocking to a devout Catholic! Most of its inhabitants were apostate from the Roman Catholic Church, having accepted the heretical Protestant teachings of Martin Luther and John Calvin. Surely Madame Guyon was not one to forsake her faith or leave the Church she loved so strongly.

What! she thought. *To complete my reprobation, shall I go to such an excess of impiety as to quit the faith through apostasy? Am I about to leave the Church and depart from the faith for which I would gladly give a thousand lives?*

This required a decision on her part. What course should she take? Stay with her grouchy old mother-in-law? Remarry? Or arrange her earthly affairs and enter a nunnery? The latter appealed to her the most. She reasoned that she could serve God best in a nunnery, hidden away from the contamination of the world. Besides, had she not already taken the marriage covenant to Christ as her own final vows? But—what if she were one who enters the religious life and fails to find God's will there? How could she serve Him under such binding circumstances? Furthermore, she doubted that this would be best for the children because it would remove her from them permanently, a resolution she found unacceptable the more she considered it.

Father Francois La Combe, a Barnabite Superior in Thonon, not far from Geneva, frequently visited the Guyon house when Monsieur Guyon was still living. A spiritual closeness existed between Father La Combe and Madame Guyon. She still regarded him as her spiritual director although she had been assigned to Monsieur Bertot. Father La Combe's advice and prayers on her behalf had helped her find faith in Christ so precious. Now she needed his help in making this important decision.

She wrote to him, designating July 22, 1680, the twelfth anniversary of her conversion, as the day he should pray for her—if the letter reached him in time. Both fasted and prayed that day. No longer depressed and downcast, Madame Guyon realized that, as hard as this state of privation was to endure at the time, she had come through it spiritually triumphant! At last she felt relieved of her long burden of sadness. Her soul was restored, as it were, to a more mature spiritual life in Christ Jesus.

Assured now that her life could be nothing less than a life of faith and total abandonment to Christ, Madame Guyon saw the straight and narrow way as a dedicated walk in which every step is regulated by one's acceptance of God's will as illuminated by the Holy Spirit. Thus it was that she continued loyal to the Roman Catholic Church while practicing the Christian faith as God revealed it to her. Looking back upon her recent years of trials and temptations, she envisioned the whole period like tunnels winding through mountains of great difficulties, opening up into a valley of blessings and the Lord's heavenly green pastures.

Soon it was obvious she would have to free herself from family obligations. Her sacred marriage to the Lord Jesus Christ required giving up all to follow Him, wherever it was His pleasure to want her. Of course it would be hard to leave the children, almost like orphans, deprived of maternal affection. Yet she could not set aside the words of a confessor-priest in Paris who had told her on their first meeting earlier in 1680: "You know that if God shows to you that He requires something of you, there is absolutely nothing in the world which ought to hinder you from doing His will. Even if you must leave your children to accomplish it, the sacrifice is necessary."

This one thing was sure. Answering the Lord's call was not the easiest undertaking. Nevertheless, she knew she had to go to Geneva. But on those occasions when she allowed herself to view the situation through human eyes, Madame Guyon found herself wondering like some of her pious acquaintances.

Could I possibly be mistaken? she would think, fearful of the uncertainties she had to face.

Her children were the only objects in life that gave Madame Guyon joy outside of her close relationship with the Lord Jesus Christ and the Church she loved so dearly. After some deliberation and much prayer, she finally persuaded herself to give her mother-in-law power of attorney over a small allowance from the family income and leave the younger boy with her. The other boy would receive proper Christian teaching and guidance with competent foster parents. Although this arrangement for the boys seemed practical, she felt uneasy at leaving the little girl. So she decided to keep the girl herself.

Impatient now to be on her way and fully aware that she might appear to be a fool in the eyes of others, still she had to go! She decided to go first to that part of France, Burgundy, which bordered the Republic of Geneva, to work among the unChristianized in the little towns nestling comfortably at the foot of the Alps. But, to settle some of the lingering questions and doubts in her mind, Madame Guyon consulted a gentleman friend about her plan. He gave his approval subject to the condition that she consult Bishop D'Aranthon of Geneva, who resided at Annecy, some twenty miles south of the city of Geneva, in the Duchy of Savoy. He even volunteered to speak to the Bishop himself on her behalf. Then it was learned that Bishop D'Aranthon was in Paris on Church business. So Madame Guyon had no difficulty securing an immediate audience with him. At last she was in the presence of one whose judgment carried some weight in the Church! Soon she would have the answer to all of her nagging doubts.

· · · · ·

> 'Twas my purpose on a day,
> To embark and sail away.
> As I climb'd the vessel's side,
> LOVE was sporting in the tide;
> "Come," He said. "Ascend—make haste,
> Launch into the boundless waste."

Many mariners were there,
Having each his separate care;
They that row'd us held their eyes
Fix'd upon the starry skies;
Others steer'd or turn'd the sails
To receive the shifting gales.

LOVE, with power divine supplied,
Suddenly my courage tried:
In a moment it was night,
Ship and skies were out of sight;
On the briny wave I lay,
Floating rushes all my stay.

Did I with resentment burn
At this unexpected turn?
Did I wish myself on shore,
Never to forsake it more?
No—"My soul," I cried, "be still;
If I must be lost, I will."

Next He hasten'd to convey
Both my frail supports away;
Seized my rushes; bade the waves
Yawn into a thousand graves.
Down I went, and sank as lead,
Ocean closing o'er my head.

Still, however, life was safe;
And I saw Him turn and laugh:
"Friend," He cried, "Adieu! lie low,
While the wintry storms shall blow;
When the spring has calm'd the main,
You shall rise, and float again."

Soon I saw Him with dismay
Spread His plumes, and soar away.
Now I mark His rapid flight;
Now He leaves my aching sight.
He is gone whom I adore,
'Tis in vain to seek Him more.

How I trembled then and fear'd
When my LOVE had disappear'd!
"Wilt Thou leave me thus," I cried,
"Whelm'd beneath the rolling tide?"
Vain attempt to reach His ear!
LOVE was gone, and would not hear.

Ah! Return and love me still;
See me subject to Thy will;
Frown with wrath, or smile with grace—
Only let me see Thy face!
Evil I have none to fear;
All is good, if Thou art near.

Yet He leaves me—cruel fate!
Leaves me in my lost estate;
Have I sinn'd? Oh, say wherein?
Tell me, and forgive my sin!
King and Lord, whom I adore,
Shall I see Thy face no more?

Be not angry—I resign
Henceforth all my will to Thine.
I consent that Thou depart,
Though Thine absence breaks my heart.
Go then, and forever, too;
All is right that Thou wilt do.

This was just what LOVE intended;
He was now no more offended;
Soon as I became a child,
LOVE return'd to me and smiled.
Never strife shall more betide
'Twixt the Bridegroom and His Bride.

—Madame Jeanne Guyon

7

To Gex—To Work for the Lord

Dressed in his stately red robes and skull cap, with a big religious medallion hanging from a chain around his neck and a crucifix dangling from his belt sash, the Bishop entered the anteroom surrounded by an air of dignity and solemn respect. He greeted Madame Guyon with a friendly handclasp as she bowed, extending the customary courtesies to a man of his ecclesiastical position and rank.

"*Bien, bien*, Madame Guyon. I have heard much about your charitable works, my good lady," the Bishop said. "But to what do I owe this surprising visit from so gracious a lady as yourself?"

Apparently the charms of a debonair gentleman were still among his attributes even though his Bishop's duties kept him amid books and papers most of the time.

"I want to have a ministry. What would you suggest for me to do, monsieur?" Madame Guyon asked after relating the details of her divine call and her immediate plans to go to that part of France,

Burgundy, bordering the Republic of Geneva, perhaps to establish a religious institution or a hospital there with some of her inherited wealth.

Of course Bishop D'Aranthon, being greatly concerned over the welfare of the poverty-stricken people in his diocese, was pleased to find a wealthy person, such as Madame Guyon, willing to aid them. A generous contribution would certainly help alleviate some of the dire poverty existing in the Geneva area. Also, he was anxious to gain recognition from the Pope. He wanted to do everything possible to convert the large numbers of new Protestants in his diocese back to Roman Catholicism. Madame Guyon's money, he mused, could help achieve these goals.

After making the sign of the cross and mumbling a quiet prayer on her behalf, the Bishop said, "As you know, I have the authority to appoint workers on missions to various districts to indoctrinate New Catholics in the faith. You, my dear lady, are an answer to my prayers. You could teach these people. You would also help the poor with your generous giving. Yes, I do believe it would be the Lord's will. You have my approval. You can go to Gex."

For this Madame Guyon was grateful even though Gex was not exactly Geneva. Gex was a small town near the southeastern tip of the Province of Burgundy, situated twelve miles northwest of the Republic of Geneva.

"I shall be happy to do exactly as you suggest, Most Reverend Father. It will give me the opportunity to serve my Lord—and that is what I want most in life," she responded.

The Bishop's one request was that she moderate her views and oral expression to conform with the dogma and the language of the Church. This had to be, because the state laws on religion demanded that everyone be extremely cautious about the use of religious terms and opinions these days. Already many deviations from the Roman Catholic faith had sprung up in Germany, Italy and Spain, and were gaining a foothold in France as well. Bishop D'Aranthon welcomed Madame Guyon to his diocese; but since he could ill afford to have difficulties either with the King or His Eminence the Pope, he hoped this wealthy woman's reputation of being "a perky religious rebel" was not going to be too hard to handle.

Shortly after leaving his presence, Madame Guyon sought the solace of her diary: "In Thee, O my God, I have found it all, and more than all! The peace which I now possess is all holy, heavenly, inexpressible. What I possessed some years ago, in the period of my spiritual enjoyment, was consolation, peace—the gift of God rather than the Giver; but now, I have been brought into such harmony with the will of God that I may now say that I possess not merely consolation, but the God of consolation; not merely peace, but the God of peace. This true peace of mind is worth all that I have so painfully undergone."

Bishop D'Aranthon was not the only person concerned with her actions. Already many persons within the Church violently opposed Madame Guyon. The most ardent resistance came from her own half-brother Father La Mothe, who threatened to exert his widespread influence as a defender of the faith and use his friendship with both King Louis XIV and the Archbishop of Paris in order to keep Madame Guyon securely under control in Paris. He regarded her desire to go to Geneva, that despised Protestant refuge, as a foolhardy and dangerous notion. The Bishop was beginning to think the same of her, but he could not afford to allow her generous donations to slip through his fingers. He would just have to keep his eye on her.

Father La Mothe even disagreed with the opinion of Bishop D'Aranthon, who had given his approval to Madame Guyon's call and assigned her to work with the New Catholics in Gex. Of course, he had no way of knowing the Bishop's true feelings. Because of his doubts about her call to the ministry, Father La Mothe found it difficult to see his sister engaging in church work as a mere lay-person. As a non-professional, she had no business meddling in official Church activities! He would find a way to stop her.

Frequently, persons who lost favor with either the Church or the state were suddenly seized and imprisoned in the Castle of Vincennes or the Bastille under orders secretly issued by the King. Knowing this, Madame Guyon took her half-brother's threats quite seriously, not doubting for one moment to what lengths he would go to stop her in what he termed "a risky venture." Like "a child of another world," as she later described herself, this thirty-three-year-old widow went forth with the call of God upon her heart and an intense desire to do God's will, not knowing exactly what the Lord required of her. Yet she was determined to go on even though adversity and oppression were bound to follow.

Weighing the matter carefully in an effort to avoid a confrontation in which she would surely lose, Madame Guyon bought passage for herself and her traveling party on the public stagecoach to a nearby place. Then to avoid suspicion, they left most of their personal property and household furnishings with her mother-in-law and other trusted friends, limiting themselves to the number of garments that they could possibly wear at one time. The only visible luggage Madame Guyon and her daughter carried when they boarded the boat that dark July night in 1681 was a small valise containing a few personal items, some books, a quill pen, ink and a supply of writing paper. In their purses they carried only enough money to assure reaching their destination. Accompanying her and her five-year-old daughter, who was at the loquaciously inquisitive age, were a lady friend named Sister Garnier and two trustworthy maidservants.

The boat moved slowly up the river that quiet, peaceful July night. Although it was warm and stuffy, the gentle summer breezes caused the trees along the water's edge to sway in a soothing, undulating manner, so different from the tenseness of those in the boat who were trying to avoid being recognized by the boat's crew. In the morning the little girl, Maria Jeanne Guyon, busied herself by pulling twigs and leaves from the willows and bushes along the river bank. Then she fastened the twigs together into the form of crosses. "After the crosses, Mama, you will be crowned," the child announced as she placed a crown of leaves and grass on her mother's head.

Since Madame Guyon looked for signs to confirm the validity of God's call, she attached special meaning to her little daughter's actions and words, regarding this incident as God's means of foretelling future events.

While enroute, Madame Guyon communed continually with her Lord, praying silently and singing songs of praise with the other ladies to pass the time. Most of the trip was made in easy steps, as they spent each night with friends or sympathetic people who had been recommended to Madame Guyon. At Corbeil, seventeen miles from Paris, Madame Guyon stopped to visit the Franciscan monk who had been instrumental in leading her to accept the Lord Jesus Christ as her personal Savior. Being now older and more mature in judging spiritual matters, the Franciscan approved her plan whole-heartedly and invoked God's blessing upon her as she set out on her assignment.

Her friend Sister Garnier left the boat at Melun, twenty-five miles southeast of Paris. The other women took a hired carriage to the beautiful city of Lyon, which is located about 240 miles southeast of Paris at the confluence of the Rhone and Saone Rivers. Between Lyon and Chambery, traveling by carriage was hard and quite dangerous. Sometimes the passengers had to get out and walk over the rocky pathway. Once the carriage broke down. Passing from one town to another, they would stop to rest at the public inn. Then they would go to the nearest church to worship until mealtime, while the little girl rested from the weariness of travel over such deteriorating, rubble-strewn roadways.

Before reaching Chambery they crossed the border between France and the Duchy of Savoy. Then on July 21, 1681, they arrived at Annecy, the residence of Bishop D'Aranthon. The next day was Saint Magdalen's Day, which held special meaning for Madame Guyon because just thirteen years before, on Saint Magdalen's Day, she had experienced a tremendous spiritual rebirth. Four years later she had given herself to the Lord in an even more serious way by signing the *Act of Consecration*, as a marriage covenant to the Lord Jesus Christ. From that day on she never ceased to hear her Blessed Savior intone those beautiful and cherished words from the Prophet Hosea: "And I will betroth thee unto Me forever; yea, I will betroth thee unto Me in righteousness, and in judgment, and in lovingkindness, and in mercies. I will even betroth thee unto Me in faithfulness; and thou shalt know the Lord."

To commemorate these two occasions, Bishop D'Aranthon said Mass for her at the tomb of Saint Francis de Sales. Here Madame Guyon renewed her spiritual vows to the Lord Jesus Christ. It was indeed a joyous and happy day for them both!

Proceeding north to Geneva, the travelers went to see the French Consul and to attend Mass, continuing on that afternoon to a small French village just beyond the Swiss border. The next day they arrived in Gex, a town situated at the foot of Mount Saint Claude in the Jura Mountains of eastern France, and twelve miles from the city of Geneva.

Without any definite plan of action except to wait for divine guidance, Madame Guyon with her little daughter and the two maidservants took up temporary residence at the House of the Sisters of Charity. So it was with peace of mind and the sweet presence of the Lord alive in her soul that Madame Guyon felt at last she was in the one place in the entire world where God wanted her to be. Happy and overflowing with supreme joy that only the Holy Spirit can impart, Madame Guyon spent hour after hour praying and communing with God—drinking His rich blessing into her soul. It was truly a time of spiritual refreshment to better prepare her for the taxing work that lay ahead in Gex.

Soon it became generally known in Paris that Madame Guyon had left the city. Father La Mothe lost no time in locating her. Conscious of her concern for her children, Father La Mothe wrote to her, deliberately lying about her mother-in-law's failing health. By doing this he hoped to alarm her enough to entice her back to Paris where he would have her incarcerated until she reneged on what appeared to him to be a foolhardy venture. But this wanton scheme failed. The call of God was so strongly fixed in her heart and soul that, at this point, absolutely nothing could cause her to turn back.

Then one day Monsieur D'Aranthon, Bishop of Geneva, came to inform her that, soon after she left Paris, her authorized spiritual director Monsieur Bertot had taken ill and died. Bertot had approved her mission. His writings, which were published shortly after his death, included some of Madame Guyon's correspondence with him on spiritual subjects. Now it was necessary for the Bishop to appoint someone in Bertot's place as Madame Guyon's spiritual director. Father Francois La Combe was named. This appointment pleased both, as Father La Combe had been a close friend of the Guyon family for a number of years already—part of that time as their spiritual director—and was completely knowledgeable of Madame Guyon's desire to serve the Lord. He was also very understanding of her views and opinions as to mental prayer, meditation, the born-again experience and the closeness of the Holy Spirit in the life of the believer.

For Madame Guyon the trip from Paris to Gex had been rigorous. Now, with the extremely hot weather, there was spoiled food and polluted water to contend with, plus hard work that Madame Guyon, a lady of wealth and refinement, was unaccustomed to. She became violently ill and it looked as if she were near death's door, languishing for days in a lethargic state of exhaustion. So the Sisters of Charity wrote to Father La Combe, asking him to come with haste to comfort her in her last hours.

Since Father La Combe was bound by vows of poverty, he had no money on this occasion to hire horse or carriage. To get to Gex to minister to his faithful charge, he walked all night. Upon entering Madame Guyon's room he laid his hands upon her fevered brow and prayed intensely for her deliverance. Instantly her temperature dropped down to normal. God had answered prayer and raised her up from near death! There was great awe and rejoicing in the sanctuary as word of this marvelous healing spread.

Of all the priests with whom she had acquaintance, only Father La Combe, her spiritual director, understood this woman's inward mystical experience. He advised her on more than one occasion to take time to pray through so that she would come to recognize God's will more fully. But Madame Guyon replied, "God will not fail to show me what course I should take, when on the one hand He finds me ready to do His commands and on the other hand He is ready to make His commands known. I leave, therefore, everything with Him, and with His providence. Thy will be done, O Lord."

Another time of spiritual enlightenment came to her when she accompanied Father La Combe to Thonon, in Savoy, to visit her young daughter, who was at that time staying with some nuns in that beautiful lake region. A storm came up as they crossed Lake Leman. But although the boat almost capsized several times in the torrential rain, they arrived safely at their destination. For twelve days Madame Guyon visited her daughter. However, her visit turned out also to be a religious retreat of great depth and spiritual maturity, for during this time God manifested Himself to her in a marvelously supernatural manner. Basking in the presence of the Lord, she renewed her close relationship with Christ and made vows of perpetual chastity, poverty and obedience, covenanting with the Lord to do whatever she knew to be the will of God, totally and without reservation. She agreed also to submit to Church authorities and to honor the Lord Jesus Christ always as her espoused Bridegroom.

Although she had found plenty to do to occupy herself since arriving in Gex, she was not completely satisfied with the situation. Her unselfish acts of charity were of such outstanding quality that Bishop D'Aranthon wrote an honest letter expressing his deep personal gratitude for the good she had done for the poor in his diocese: mixing ointment, cutting bandages, mopping floors and tending the sick. She did all this in addition to teaching children the rudiments of reading, writing, and the catechism. Yet during this time that inner voice kept reminding her that this was not exactly what God had called her to do.

She returned to Gex convinced that she had a mission and a message to give to the world. To the professing Christian, her message was the doctrine of justification and sanctification through the atoning work of Jesus Christ. This was based upon the fact that, as born-again believers, they possessed the God of forgiveness and of holiness, which made justification and sanctification their particular privilege. Such a sentiment struck Roman Catholics, especially the clergy, with fear and astonishment! This was exactly what Martin Luther, the reformer, had proclaimed when he wrote his Ninety-five Theses against the practice of penance and indulgences being promoted and sold by the Roman Catholic Church authorities. Tolerance of religious sentiments such as these for a devout Roman Catholic were unthinkable, bordering on heresy. Ceremonial observance, acts of devotion and penance, prescribed rituals and papal law characterized the Roman Catholic way of life. So when anyone began to express varying views on what had been established Church doctrine, it caused the flames of revival and opposition to blaze and spread out. With her affable voice raised to proclaim God's Word as it was revealed to her by the Holy Spirit there at the foot of the towering Swiss Alps, Madame Guyon's message reached back into high places in that glamorous, worldly city of Paris from which she had begun her spiritual journey.

Some people believed and rejoiced in the truth. Some reproached her for daring to say things which appeared to be contrary to the set doctrine of the Church. Some disapproved but said very little. Others were enraged enough to condemn Madame Guyon and all she set her hand to do, threatening to put to naught this woman and her ministry.

One could say that things had gone rather well until this point in time. Bishop D'Aranthon knew of the good this woman was doing for his parish and his people. Still he felt compelled, in the performance of his clerical duty, to denounce the irregular doctrinal statements Madame Guyon was proposing and promoting among even the most devout Roman Catholics. Wherever she went, she seemed impelled by the Holy Spirit to recommend Jesus as the Savior from all one's sins, past and present—even to those who already professed a strong belief in Him. She urged those born-again Christians to be aware that

God can and does give His Holy Spirit of truth, meekness, gentleness, longsuffering, purity and holiness to all who desire to be His humble witnesses. These are the truths that the eminent Bishop D'Aranthon later declared were so irregular as to cause him to label Madame Jeanne Guyon a heretic, instead of the devout Roman Catholic she supposed herself to be.

In those days of guilt by association, nearly everyone connected with Madame Guyon was suspected of holding similar irregular views. Father Francois La Combe, her spiritual director, was one of these unfortunates. It was during their earlier acquaintance that Father La Combe had been led by her council and concern into his first experience with the Blessed Holy Spirit. Madame Guyon had a deep concern for his innermost spiritual development and Christian maturity. Linked together by a common bond of faith in the power of Jesus Christ to save from sin, to sanctify and to make perfect the believer, Father La Combe and Madame Guyon prayed for each other's sanctification and spiritual growth. The two often found their situations reversed, with Madame Guyon counseling the unhappy, harassed priest! Later, both met with harsh rebuke, opposition and, ultimately, imprisonment because of La Combe's association with her and because of their intense and intimate love for God that took precedence over the petty edicts of their superiors.

Until now, Father La Combe could intellectually accept the doctrine of sanctification by faith in Christ as our Sanctifier (rather than through penance), as something he needed, but he still attached much importance to certain emotional feelings as both outward and inward evidences of true fellowship with the Lord. How hard it was for this honest, sincere priest, an astute Bible scholar, to walk by faith alone. He kept looking for things that satisfied human logic and reason even though he knew spiritual things cannot always be explained rationally. Self-renunciation and simplicity of faith were, at that time, just too simple for this learned and gifted man of God to accept.

To be truly sanctified in the Lord Jesus Christ and to reach toward ultimate spiritual maturity, Madame Guyon taught that one must die to self so as to become totally enveloped in the love of God and to be dependent upon God's grace and mercy for all His blessings. As Father La Combe progressed spiritually, he honestly accepted Madame Guyon's explanations on faith, prayer and holiness. His soul yearned to do the express will of God more than ever before in his long years of studying for the priesthood, preaching the gospel, and ministering to the people of his parish.

After Bishop D'Aranthon denounced Madame Guyon as a heretic, he set about to trap Father La Combe by his own words. In an attempt to do this deceitful thing, the Bishop invited Father La Combe to preach in his diocese. La Combe chose for his sermon text Psalm 45:13, "The King's daughter is all glorious within: her clothing is of wrought gold." In his sermon he likened the King to the Lord Jesus Christ and the King's daughter to the genuinely born-again believers as the Lord's Bride collectively. In so doing he proposed to point out the difference between a religious experience consisting of the observance of ceremony, ritual and penances, and that which is of the Holy Spirit of God—possessing and filling the soul of the believer with pure love and holiness, like a cup of toddy on a cold winter's day.

Of course Bishop D'Aranthon declared that Father La Combe's sermon was full of doctrinal irregularities and errors of interpretation. As he drew up his paper exposing the alleged heretical character of Father La Combe's sermon, Bishop D'Aranthon was convinced the ecclesiastical authority in Rome would find definite evidence of heresy in the eight propositions he set forth against this priest. He sent the thesis to Rome immediately; but the expected response never came, surprising him and causing him to wonder about the state of the modern-day religious world.

The Bishop was convinced that Madame Guyon was the cause of Father La Combe's erroneous doctrine. Although he had approved of this wealthy widow coming into his diocese, he never expected her to teach dogmatics so passionately. Naturally, he blamed her for the spread of diversionary thinking wherever he found it in his diocese. This had to stop at once. But at this point he did not know what to do about his dilemma, until a young ecclesiastic came up with what seemed like the perfect solution.

This young man had been intimately involved with one of Madame Guyon's maidservants, and he was still angry with her for breaking up their passionate relationship. So he approached the Bishop with a scheme that would put Madame Guyon out of the way and still make her inherited wealth available to the Church. He suggested that the Bishop consider taking her annual income, because of her voluntary vow of poverty, as a donation to a religious house of which she would be the Prioress. Upon hearing this well-planned scheme, Bishop D'Aranthon went immediately to Madame Guyon with the proposition. He tried his best to convince her that being the Prioress of a religious community in Gex would give added scope and expression to her personal commitment to the Lord and would be a means whereby she could put her money to good use also. But Madame Guyon would hear of no such thing.

Because she had never become a novitiate she felt herself unqualified to be a Prioress. Besides, she knew that if she stayed in Gex in this capacity she would be putting herself in opposition to God's ultimate plan. So she refused the Bishop's excited offer.

Not at all satisfied with her refusal, Bishop D'Aranthon went to Father La Combe for his help. As her spiritual director, Father La Combe had the authority to force her to accept the Bishop's proposal. The Bishop's argument was that, by having Father La Combe persuade Madame Guyon to do this, he would only be reminding her of the vows of poverty and obedience she had already made. However, Father La Combe easily saw through these noble espousals to the scheme lurking behind the Bishop's offer. He could never, in good conscience, take unfair advantage of anyone by making such heavy demands as this. Upon hearing his refusal to help, Bishop D'Aranthon threatened to degrade and suspend him. Still Father La Combe stood his ground, saying, "Sir, I am ready, not only to suffer suspension, but even death, rather than do anything against my conscience." However, he did inform Madame Guyon about his interview with the Bishop and allowed her to decide for herself what to do.

Reacting like a little boy taking his toys away from a former playmate, Bishop D'Aranthon ordered Madame Guyon out of his diocese! Angered and deeply hurt by all this, Bishop D'Aranthon never forgave Father La Combe for what he termed rank insubordination by refusing to use his authority against Madame Guyon. Perhaps the Bishop was jealous of this woman's extremely acute ability and influence; or his sin and haughty manners may have kept him from accepting spiritual enlightenment from a woman. Now he saw Madame Guyon's religious views, and those of Father La Combe, as diversions from the truth and too closely allied to Protestantism rather than Roman Catholic orthodoxy. His stand against them now became more direct and less subtle. Certain other ecclesiastics, including her half-brother Father La Mothe, also joined in expressing open opposition against them.

However, Madame Guyon was so thoroughly convinced of the importance of possessing the Holy Spirit, being sanctified by faith in the blood of Jesus, and living intimately with God in the Spirit that she could not stop telling others the joyous news about her resurrected Savior. Especially upsetting to the Church authorities were her teachings which emphasized the clear difference between ritualistic forms of worship and true spiritual reality, plus the need to encourage literacy so that all Christians could read the Bible for themselves. Wherever she found a person who would listen, she would endeavor to explain these views which differed from that of the established Church. Bishop D'Aranthon was one who listened and later used her own words as the ground of offense when he brought his charge of heresy against her before an inquisition hearing.

From now on Madame Guyon faced one trial after another. The fat was beginning to hit the fire. *In* the Roman Catholic Church but not *of* it, Madame Guyon worked for the Lord and gave her money generously to the Church. Exposed as she was to all manner of personal inconveniences and attacks, she rightly described herself as "a child of another world." Like the Lord's first apostles, this woman had received the Holy Spirit and went about preaching the gospel, proclaiming the good news that Jesus saves and heals and satisfies the soul in its quest for the Creator. In spite of all this, she maintained that she was a faithful Roman Catholic and would never turn her back upon the Lord's call or His Church.

At this time her teachings and opinions on religious matters were denounced publicly as heretical by the Bishop. At the same time, her character and morals were attacked with false words and gross calumny.

In order not to cause herself or Father La Combe any further difficulties, Madame Guyon decided to

visit her six-and-a-half-year-old daughter Maria
Jeanne, who was still at the Ursuline Convent in
Thonon, Savoy. Of course, the little girl was delighted to see her mother again. But during this visit
the girl became sick with smallpox. Madame Guyon
sent for Father La Combe to come before going to
Rome on Church business. He came immediately
and prayed for the child's rapid recovery.

· · · · ·

"In God I found with increase everything which
I had lost previously. . . . But when God gave back to
me that love which I had supposed to have lost, although I had never ceased to love Him, He restored
the powers of perception and thought also. . . . The
understanding, as well as the heart, seemed to have
received an increased, renewed capacity from God;
so much so that others noticed it, and spoke of its
greatly increased power as it manifested itself in me.
It seemed to me that I experienced something of the
state which the apostles were in, after they had received the Holy Ghost. I knew, I comprehended, I
was enabled to do intellectually as well as physically, everything which was requisite. I had every
sort of thing, and no want of anything. I remembered that fine passage which is found in the apoc-
ryphal book called the Wisdom of Solomon. Speaking of WISDOM, the writer, in the seventh chapter,
says, 'I prayed, and understanding was given me; I
called upon God, and the spirit of Wisdom came to
me. I loved her above health and beauty, and chose
to have her instead of light; for the light that cometh

from her never goeth out. All good things together came to me with her, and innumerable riches in her hands.' Wisdom came to me, too, in following Christ. When Jesus Christ, the Eternal Wisdom, is formed in the soul, after the death of the first Adam, it finds in Him all good things communicated to it."

—Madame Jeanne Guyon

8

She Begins
Her Religious Writing

After returning from Rome, where he had been on Church business, Father La Combe granted Madame Guyon permission for a spiritual retreat at the Ursuline Convent in Thonon. In fact, he was quick to grant her request, hoping that her stay in Thonon would allow time for the storm clouds aroused by Bishop D'Aranthon's anger to subside.

While in Thonon she engaged in worship, prayer and fasting in a concerted effort to find the Lord's will. It was here that she felt a strong impulse to write. But thinking that she had nothing special to write about, she immediately dismissed the notion. When she finally realized that she must write, she told Father La Combe of her intentions. He also reacted with surprise, asking the same question, "But what will you write?"

To this Madame Guyon replied in all sincerity, "I don't know, nor do I desire to know. I leave it entirely to God to direct me."

As it turned out in the years that followed, words flowed from this woman's pen swiftly, copiously and impetuously, like water released from a lake no longer dammed. With no access to reference books and little opportunity to study, Madame Guyon set about to write religious tracts, pamphlets and Bible commentaries with the Holy Spirit guiding her thoughts and practically dictating the words.

While in the Ursuline Convent she experienced a continuously vivid series of visions, revelations and prophecies. Her life was characterized by great simplicity of faith and spiritual power. After her conversion she led many into the born-again experience. Now that her soul had experienced this deeper, richer, fuller spiritual awakening which she called "death to self," she felt compelled to lead others into the same holy walk of faith. Her soul seemed to vibrate with the unction and power of the Holy Spirit, and she radiated it outward like a warm sun in a world of darkness. Sanctification by faith in Jesus as Sanctifier, and victory over self through His Spirit, made her even more conscious of her mystical espousal to the Lord Jesus Christ, the crucified, risen and coming Savior of her soul.

A revival broke out in Thonon and the nearby town of Lausanne, across the lake, as Madame Guyon continued her successful witnessing in Thonon. On one occasion when her maidservant was very sick, Madame Guyon simply spoke to the girl, saying, "Get up. In the name of Jesus you are no longer sick." The girl stood to her feet, instantly cured by the miraculous healing power of God. Wherever Madame Guyon went, she attracted a large following. People came seeking religious instruction, prayer and salvation. Never could she turn people away when they came for help and encouragement. She talked and prayed with hungry souls during the day and did her writing long into the night. Then she would follow up their visits with correspondence in those cases which she felt required more counseling.

In 1683, while in Thonon, she wrote *The Torrents*, a small book in which she described the process of the soul as it reaches out toward God. This writing must be interpreted as a recitation of the inward spiritual experience she herself enjoyed. She likened the true outpouring of God's grace and mercy to a torrent which begins in the mountains and high hills as a trickling stream and rolls toward the great ocean of God's infinite love in the sea far below. It illustrates the deep inner peace that results from putting all one's desires into God's hand and ultimately finding fulfillment in Jesus as one's will becomes totally submitted to His.

Throughout this time Bishop D'Aranthon still could not accept Madame Guyon's refusal to return to Gex to establish a religious house. Visiting her a second time in Thonon, he did his best to make her agree to his terms. Her refusal only infuriated him and brought more persecution and hardship to both herself and her dear friend Father La Combe.

Apparently the dampness of this lake region aggravated her congenitally poor health, so she decided to find another place of ministry. Turin, capital of the Duchy of Savoy, seemed to be the place. On this trip Madame Guyon, her young daughter and a maidservant were accompanied by a theologian, a young lad and Father La Combe, who was on his way to Verceil on Church business. They parted company in Turin, leaving Madame Guyon and her companions at the home of the Marchioness of Prunai, who was the sister of the Chief Secretary of State to His Royal Highness. After sufficient time to convalesce, Madame Guyon found herself busy as usual, witnessing, praying and writing as the Holy Spirit enabled her.

During these months unfounded rumors about Madame Guyon caused much notoriety. Her half-brother Father La Mothe and Bishop D'Aranthon of Geneva were the dominant leaders in this attempt to discredit her as a devilish heretic. The Bishop asked other bishops, clergymen and priests to de-nounce her in their parishes. Besides this, he or-dered her books and tracts to be burned publicly in every diocese where he had influence. These men would stop at nothing in their determination to dis-credit her. The Bishop also launched a letter-writ-ing campaign, denouncing her as a tool of Satan. Forgetting the good she had done for his poverty-stricken people, he continued to accuse her, judging her every move.

A prophetic dream prepared her for what lay ahead. So it was not a total surprise that when Fa-ther La Combe arrived back at Turin, he ordered her to return to Paris immediately. He suggested that they travel together as far as Grenoble, France, where she could spend some time with a lady-friend before go-ing on to Paris. Once there, however, she decided to heed a warning given her by this friend and not, at least for the time being, to go any further. She would stay in Grenoble where she saw her help was needed.

Grenoble was a rough, ungodly city in the diocese ruled by Bishop La Camas. It had the reputation of being much more in need of missionary workers than was China. Wickedness and sinful pleasures permeated people's pastimes. Apparently the pastor-priests and spiritual directors in the area were not giving the needed spiritual guidance to their people. So many needed the simple Christ-centered message of the gospel, and they started to seek out Madame Guyon for spiritual advice and prayer when it became known that she was in the city.

For the next two years she counseled and ministered during the day and did her writing at night, exactly as she had in Thonon. Always Madame Guyon gave the praise and glory to God for what He did through her, never claiming credit for herself. She said repeatedly, "It is Thou, O my God, who did all these things!"

The Holy Spirit gave her the gift of discernment and the perceptive wisdom she needed to understand the condition of each individual's soul, so that she was able to give each one the Scripture portions and the advice he needed. Again, she became the object of general attention and curiosity. Earnest Christians began to seek the deeper spiritual experience this woman lived and taught and wrote about. Even monks, priests, nuns and bishops came for counsel and prayer. As a result, revivals based on her religious teachings broke out in many places.

She began working on her *Bible Commentaries* in

Grenoble. For about six months, without referring to anything other than her French Bible, she wrote with a prodigious swiftness in the quiet of the night, squinting by the flickering light of several candles. At times her hand could scarcely move fast enough to put down all that the Holy Spirit dictated. It was as if she saw with the eye of her mind and wrote down as much as she possibly could while the inspiration was there. Her published writings became popular with the Quakers, whose religion, because of persecution, had become personal and contemplative. Many theological scholars describe Madame Guyon's *Bible Commentaries* as the most notable and inspiring devotional commentaries ever written, the equivalent of a modern best seller. These were later published and distributed throughout Europe.

Here, too, she wrote an inspirational book which caused heated disputes among Church officials. In this book, *A Short and Easy Method of Prayer*, translated into English and today published under the title *Experiencing the Depths of Jesus Christ*, she advocated praying directly to God in the name of Jesus Christ, thus by-passing the Blessed Virgin Mary, Church-approved saints, and those prescribed methods of prayer set forth by Roman Catholic tradition and papal law. What heresy! It could not go unnoticed by Church authorities! Brilliant theologians and churchmen took their stand for or against Madame Guyon's religious opinions on the subject. In some places, public book burnings were held in an effort to stamp out her popular teaching on prayer, which questioned so much of the Church's intermediary office. In her own experience Madame Guyon had learned that she could go directly to God the Father in prayer and that her prayer would be heard. She was convinced that praying to the Blessed Virgin Mary or to the saints was an unnecessary intermediate step. Prayer, being a personal communication with the Lord Jesus Christ, should not be controlled by rules and regulations as it was within the Roman Catholic Church. She also felt that religious services from a priest, such as saying Masses and novenas on one's behalf, should not have a price tag on them. Rather, she taught that in order to pray the effectual fervent prayer of a righteous man one's prayer life should be free and directed by the Holy Spirit.

Because of her published writings, Madame Guyon's fame spread throughout most of Europe. But all was not well. Trouble started at Grenoble when the Jesuit order began their propaganda against Jansenism and mysticism, as well as against all forms of Protestantism rampant in the land. Claiming that Madame Guyon did not know her proper place as a woman and had no business going about disturbing souls by attempting to interpret the Bible and instruct people on spiritual matters, the Jesuits denounced Madame Guyon as an extremely dangerous person—perhaps a sorceress in league with the Devil himself. Her enemies accused her of heresy, sorcery, and performing magic—all serious crimes against both Church and the state.

Bishop La Camas of Grenoble was aware of the zealousness of the Jesuit order. Although he had been tolerant of Madame Guyon, he knew it was risky for her to remain in his diocese. As a political man, he did not want to get involved in the controversy her ministry was causing with the Church authorities. Therefore he felt it necessary to persuade her to go to Marseilles—out of his jurisdiction—in case charges were brought against her.

In the spring of 1686, Madame Guyon left her daughter in a religious boarding home in Grenoble. Then she, her maidservant Mademoiselle La Gautiere, and another young girl left secretly by boat, traveling down the Isere and Rhone rivers, and arrived in Marseilles after a difficult trip. Already rumors about her had reached the city, and by that very afternoon there was a big uproar, almost a street riot, over her arrival.

Madame Guyon had been harassed by her enemies from Paris to Gex, from Gex to Thonon, from Thonon to Turin, from Turin to Grenoble, and on to Marseilles. Most of the opposition concerned her book *A Short and Easy Method of Prayer*. So she decided to see the Bishop of Marseilles and voluntarily lay the little book before him. He read it and liked it. Thus it was by his personal invitation that Madame Guyon stayed in the city eight days, ministering in homes and helping people find God's joy and peace. Then she decided to go on to Nice, in the Duchy of Savoy, where her stay was surprisingly uneventful.

Because of a desire to revisit her friend the Marchioness of Prunai, in Turin, she had traveled eastward to Nice. However, since passage by public conveyance from Nice through the Maritime Alps to

Turin was difficult, she was advised to go by ship to Savona, a seaport some eighty miles up the Mediterranean coast, and from there to take a coach inland to Turin. But what should have been a day's voyage turned out to be eleven days of life-threatening struggles against the stormy sea. They finally came ashore at Genoa, where they were confronted by angry people who disliked all Frenchmen.

Detained in Genoa several days in the midst of hostile people, her money nearly gone, Madame Guyon was quick to accept transportation inland to Verceil on a litter supported by two lame mules driven by a brutal man. It was on this seventy-mile trip that robbers approached the traveling group, innkeepers turned them away, and the women faced other frightening and dangerous experiences.

In Verceil, Madame Guyon was met by her longtime friend Father La Combe. Having returned from Paris, Father La Combe was now working in Verceil and was highly regarded by the Bishop.

Madame Guyon's stay in Verceil stretched out over several months, during which time she enjoyed the friendship of both the Bishop of Verceil and Father La Combe. The Bishop desired that both Madame Guyon and her friend the Marcheoness of Prunai reside in his jurisdiction. He even sent Father La Combe to Turin to persuade the Marchioness and her daughter to come to Verceil, promising to establish a religious society for her there. It was here at Verceil that Madame Guyon continued working on writing her *Bible Commentaries* and her remarks on *The Apocalypse*.

When she finally felt it necessary to go on to Paris, she took the usual route through Turin and over Mount Cenis pass. In Turin she revisited the Marchioness of Prunai, who was overjoyed to see her once again. At Chambery, a Savoyan town near the French border, she and her half-brother Father La Mothe met. He was cordial to her; but in her heart Madame Guyon did not fully trust him. From Chambery she went on to Grenoble, where she located her ten-year-old daughter and the maidservant she had left with the girl. From there, accompanied now by Father La Combe, they headed north toward Paris.

Though still not knowing what might lie ahead for her in Paris, Madame Guyon proceeded on, determined to do nothing except what she believed to be God's will. So it was that after five years of ministry elsewhere, Madame Guyon returned to Paris—almost as secretively as she had departed—arriving there on July 21, 1686, the eve of Saint Magdalen's Day. She had heard the voice of the Lord and she had done her best to obey His call. She had been God's instrument to make plain the simple truths of the gospel. As a result, many souls had come to know the Lord Jesus Christ as their Savior, and many believers had been led into a deeper, richer, fuller spiritual experience. Her Christian witness, intercessory prayer and inspirational writings, like pebbles tossed into a pond, had spread out in all directions to touch and influence thousands of men and women for Christ.

· · · · ·

"One must not judge of the servants of God by what their enemies say of them, nor by their being oppressed under calumnies without any resources. Jesus Christ expired under painful pangs. God uses the like conduct toward His dearest servants, to render them conformable to His Son, in whom He is always well pleased and so disposed. But few place that conformity where it ought to be. It is not in voluntary pains or austerities but in those which are suffered in a submission ever equal to the will of God, in a renunciation of our whole selves, to the end that God may be our ALL in ALL, conducting us according to His views and not our own, which are generally opposite to His. All perfection consists in this entire conformity with Jesus Christ, not in shining which worldly men esteem. It will only be seen in eternity who are the true friends of God. Nothing pleases Him but Jesus Christ, and that which bears His mark of character."

—Madame Jeanne Guyon

9

Persecution Starts

Scarcely had she arrived back in Paris when she discovered a plot woven against Father Francois La Combe and herself.

Now politically ambitious and close to both the Archbishop of Paris and King Louis XIV, Father La Mothe was in a position to throw suspicion on those of "unorthodox belief" whose arrest might advance his own cause. Besides stirring up the Jesuits against Madame Guyon, he had succeeded in strongly aligning the Barnabite Order in Paris against Father La Combe, even though La Combe was of the same order. Father La Mothe harbored an unforgiving spirit in his heart against his half-sister, as he never could accept the fact that none of her inherited wealth had come into his hands. At this particular time, Father La Mothe needed funds to rebuild a wall in his convent. He knew Madame Guyon had entrusted a sum of money to Father La Combe as a stipend for a young girl from Gex for her dowry upon entering a nunnery. He felt certain that he could persuade Madame Guyon to give him this money, which he would then be able to use as he wished. So, while flattering her to her face and making an outward expression of concern for her personal safety, Father La Mothe was actually conspiring against her, implying that there had been indiscreet and improper conduct between her and Father La Combe. Of course, such a thing was absolutely untrue and unfounded; yet the rumor, once begun, went a long distance before coming to a halt.

Father La Mothe's jealousy over Madame Guyon's money caused him to oppose her; whereas his lashing out at Father La Combe, once a personal friend, sprang entirely from revenge. Father La Combe had advised her against giving in to her half-brother's demands for money, which he claimed bordered on blackmail. In retaliation, Father La Mothe and the Barnabites of Paris combined their wits and resources to implicate both Father La Combe and Madame Jeanne Guyon as heretics on the grounds that their views on some topics were similar to those expressed by the already-condemned Michael de Molinos of Spain, who had been imprisoned in Rome by a papal order the year before. Consequently, Father La Combe was arrested on October 3, 1687, on information personally supplied to the Judge of the Ecclesiastical Court by Father La Mothe. He was then imprisoned in the Bastille, and later transferred by order of King Louis XIV to a place of confinement in Lourdes; then to the Castle of Vincennes near Paris; and still later to the Castle of Oleron.

Father La Combe's writing, *An Analysis of Mental Prayer*, was officially condemned by the authorities of the Roman Catholic Church on September 4, 1688, almost a year after he was first imprisoned in the cold dungeon of the Bastille. Just before his death in 1714 he was moved to a hospital for the mentally disturbed in Charenton, having spent a total of twenty-seven years in the inhumane confines of prison after prison.

In an attempt to bring about a degree of unity in the faith and to re-establish Roman Catholicism as the state religion in France, King Louis XIV in 1685 had revoked the Edict of Nantes (made in 1598 by King Henry IV) which granted toleration and protection to French Protestants and all religious free-thinkers. Determined to stamp out heresies and Protestantism at any costs and to put himself in a favorable light with the Pope in Rome, King Louis employed his political power and France's military strength against those who deviated from Roman Catholic doctrine and tradition. He ordered soldiers to break up religious assemblies of Protestants throughout all of his domain, trying to coerce people back into the Roman Catholic Church. It was this religio-political situation that was causing all the present trouble.

Now thirty-eight years old, Madame Guyon was still youthful enough to be challenged by the cause of Christ yet wise enough to have benefitted from past experiences. Most importantly, this woman was deeply and desperately in love with Jesus, her Heavenly Bridegroom, to whom she was espoused in spiritual union. Because she had proclaimed the truth of God's Word to poor farmers in their chalets in the Jura Mountains, revival had spread like a blazing forest fire; and it had occurred again and again as this "child of another world" journeyed about from one place to another, sharing her spiritual wisdom.

Already her fame had spread throughout France. Her religious books and tracts were being sold and read everywhere on the European continent. The official religious world was well aware of her popular religious views and experience.

Because of her teachings, Madame Guyon was considered by many to be the promoter of a "new spirituality" which, if allowed to spread, could subvert the practices common to the Roman Catholic tradition. Already the subject of great controversy, she was now suspected of what was politely termed "heretical tendencies." Because her religious views were similar to those of Michael de Molinos, the Spanish Quietist, King Louis XIV could see the germs of deviation growing in his own kingdom and even within the doors of the established Church. Something had to be done, he was convinced, to stop this woman forever!

One day Father La Mothe met her in a Paris church with a scheming proposition. Because he had helped to weave the plot against Madame Guyon and Father La Combe in the first place, he was knowledgeable of the charges then pending against her. But now he approached her as a loving and caring brother, supposedly to warn her of imminent danger and to assist her in avoiding certain arrest and humiliation.

"My sister," he said, "the time has come. You must decide to leave Paris forever. Go home to Montargis where you will be safe. There are heavy allegations against you of such a nature that there seems to be no other course for you. You are even charged with high crimes against the throne. I fear for you. Please go while you can."

"If I am guilty of such crimes, I cannot be too severely punished for them," Madame Guyon replied. "Let my punishment come. I cannot run in the face of adversity. I have made an open profession of dedicating myself to the Lord entirely. If I have done things offensive to God—whom I love and would cause to be loved by the whole world, even at the expense of my life—then I ought, by my punishment, to be made a special example to the world; but if I am innocent, fleeing would prejudice my claims to innocence. I will stay right where I am. I have no cause to run and therefore I will not!"

Not anticipating such a response, Father La Mothe became enraged and departed, making violent threats against her and the children because of her "stupid" stubbornness. From then on, there was no end to what Father La Mothe could and did do to terrify Madame Guyon. Using every imaginable device to malign her character, he accused her of all manner of misconduct and erroneous views. He openly threatened to inform on her both to the Church hierarchy and to politically ambitious officials who were urging arrest and detention as the only effective means of restricting her influence.

Two uneventful months passed before her case finally came before the Archbishop of Paris for a hearing. However, the Archbishop was already well aware that Madame Guyon's total reliance upon faith in Jesus Christ for salvation, sanctification and spiritual liberty tended to subvert the established practices and traditions of the Roman Catholic Church. As a learned churchman, he knew that such doctrinal intepretations must not be allowed to grow, particularly in the fertile soil that was the majority of the French population. The Roman Church could soon find itself trapped into accommodating itself to some form of Protestantism. This it absolutely could not afford to do. So, having no other alternative, he promptly condemned Madame Guyon publicly for promoting heresies.

Soon afterward the Archbishop of Paris published a paper entitled *An Ordinance and Pastoral Instructions* justifying his judgment and decision in the matter. But because he had no authority to imprison anyone without the signature of the King, he first took the transcript of the case and certain evidence to King Louis himself, requesting that an order be issued at once for Madame Guyon's arrest and imprisonment— as a heretic and a menace to the Church. Naturally, from these documents King Louis concluded that the evidence weighed heavily against Madame Guyon. He issued, without delay, orders for her immediate arrest. This occurred about three months after her dear friend Father La Combe had been sent to the Bastille.

The charges against Madame Guyon were extensive. They included the promulgation of heretical opinions on religious subjects, holding and encouraging private religious assemblies, deviation from traditional forms of confession and prayer, departure from the veneration of saints, and penning a dangerous book containing religious sentiments similar to *The Spiritual Guide* of Michael de Molinos. But as to the latter charge, Madame Guyon had neither met Michael de Molinos nor had any correspondence with him. Yet at the trial, witnesses and letters were produced as evidence linking the two together. The result: Her writings were declared to be heretical—to be suppressed immediately.

Like Martin Luther, who dared to point out in his *Ninety-five Theses* certain errors and false practices of the Roman Catholic Church, Madame Guyon taught that justification came by faith in Jesus Christ alone. And sanctification, too. In fact, it was her reliance upon personal faith in the crucified and resurrected Jesus as the foundation of the Christian life—simple, unembellished faith—that the Roman Catholic Church found to be the most objectionable. That she refused to adore the saints, particularly the Blessed Virgin Mary, was true. She explained it in this manner: "The beginners in the Christian life, the servants rather than the sons of God, might possibly have some need of the influence and intercession of the saints; but the spouse obtains everything she needs without such helps."

Until now her writings had been questioned and criticized by various clergymen, but none had yet been condemned officially by the Pope in Rome as heretical. Madame Guyon claimed that her book *A Short and Easy Method of Prayer* was merely an effort to explain how to use the Lord's Prayer to best advantage. But the storm clouds had already surged in as a gale from the horizon, and her sun was in danger of disappearing from view. Attempting to explain her intentions at this point was futile.

· · · · ·

"How wonderful, O my God, at this, as at many other times, has been Thy divine protection over me! How many perils have I passed through in going over mountains, and on clinging to the edges of steep and terrible cliffs! How often hast Thou checked the foot of the mule, already slipping over the precipice! How often have I been exposed to be thrown headlong from frightful heights into hideous torrents, which, though rolling in chasms far below our shrinking sight, forced us to hear them by their horrible noise! Thou, O God, didst guard me in such imminent dangers. When the dangers were most manifest, then was my faith in Thee strongest manifest. In Thee my soul trusted. I felt that if it were Thy will that I should be dashed headlong down the rocks, or drowned in the waters, or brought to the end of my life in any other way, it would all be well—the will of God, whatever it might be in relation to me, making everything equal."

—Madame Jeanne Guyon

10

First Imprisonment

Early on the morning of January 29, 1688, Madame Guyon was arrested and committed by the King's order to the Convent of the Visitation of Saint Marie in the Parisian suburb of Antoine. This particular site was selected for her detention because the Mother Superior was most cooperative in carrying out the King's orders to the letter concerning persons put in her convent for custodial care.

Barely recovered from her long bout with illness that winter, Madame Guyon was still weak and could hardly walk, even with the aid of a cane. Under the circumstances of her commitment, Madame Guyon expected to have her twelve-year-old daughter and a maidservant with her. She had agreed to the commitment believing that it amounted to nothing more than a period of detention while her case was under review. But when the coach accompanied by members of the King's Guard arrived at the convent, the Prioress said that the orders allowed no accommodations for the girl and the maidservant. They would have to go home. The King's orders stipulated that Madame Jeanne Guyon was to be locked up alone and deprived of all visitors except by special written arrangement.

These were rather severe restrictions for one who had agreed to be detained, but all was not lost to this resourceful woman. The time spent at Saint Marie's Convent proved, in many ways, to be the most productive period of her life.

Being imprisoned did not stop her working for the Lord! She was never idle within the confines afforded her. In spite of all the mistreatment and deprivation which she endured so courageously, Madame Guyon found her soul always basking in the presence of the Lord. To the person called to do God's will there should never be a time or place in which it is impossible to obey the Lord's commandments. The spiritual joy and victory visible on her pockmarked face showed the other young women and nuns in the convent that she was truly a Christian, even though they had little or no opportunity to mingle.

In a letter smuggled out to a friend, Madame Guyon gave a few details about this first imprisonment:

> It is no news to you that I am a wretched prisoner, and always kept under lock and key; and that, except for the women who have charge of the room in which I am shut up, I am not permitted to speak to anyone unless it be by special arrangement. I am afflicted with a hell on earth, but my firm trust in God does not waver. And will not one, madame, whom I know is not indifferent to my situation, impart to me the great consolation of knowing that she has given her whole heart to the Savior?

Oh, how sad it is to see how much opposition there is to the religion of the heart! I see and hear so much of it that I am sometimes overwhelmed and confounded, and hardly know what I am saying or doing. I have, however, the consolation which is given to every heart that has truly found God.

Her sorry living quarters consisted of nothing more than a small, upper-story room with one outside window and a door that was always locked or barred from the outside. The small window remained open to let in fresh air and natural light. At the same time it admitted the clammy night dampness, morning dew, the rain or snow, and in warm weather, pesky bugs. When it was not raining or snowing, the sun beat down upon that side of the building, making the little room unbearably hot—a bake oven, in fact. Needless to say, under these conditions it wasn't long before Jeanne was again plagued with a persistent fever, chest pains and a violent cough. Her jailor-nun regarded her as a mentally disturbed person, a hypocrite and a pronounced heretic, but when Madame Guyon became so sick that it seemed likely she would die, the Prioress finally showed some compassion. Disregarding the terms of the King's orders, the Prioress ordered the services of a physician and a maidservant for Madame Guyon. This occurred in June 1688.

It was here at Saint Marie's Convent that she started writing her autobiography, a task which her spiritual director had assigned to her. He suggested that she put into written form an account of her spiritual experiences. Resignation, spiritual victory, inner peace and joy—none of which were dependent upon circumstances or her present environment—so encompassed her every moment that she made this typical entry into her autobiography: "Completed thus far—on this, the 22nd day of August 1688. I am now forty years of age, and in prison: a place which I love and cherish, as I find it sanctified by the Lord."

To one friend she wrote:

> If I were a criminal condemned to death, they could not easily give more rigorous orders concerning my being. . . . O my friend, aim higher and ever higher still! What would I not suffer to see you wholly delivered from the inward power of sin! Without ceasing I fervently pray to God that He Himself may be your WAY and TRUTH and LIFE, and that He may establish you in the supreme blessedness of pure love.

> Was not our beloved Savior looked upon and denounced in the same manner? Is it a hard matter to walk in His footsteps, and to suffer as He suffered? When I am thinking about these things I sometimes find my heart, in its perplexity, looking up and saying, "Judge me, O God, and plead my cause, for it is just!"

Being denied visitors and the companionship of other residents, she filled her solitary hours with prayer, Bible reading, spiritual songs and letter writing. The following letter, quoted almost in its entirety, is typical of her efforts, by means of correspondence, to give spiritual help to souls:

Madame, I can assure you that it is a great pleasure to me to witness the manifestations of God's mercy toward you, and to see the progress of your soul in religion. It is my soulful prayer that God may bring to a completion the work which He has begun within you. No doubt He will, if you continue ever faithful. Oh the unspeakable happiness, madame, of belonging to Jesus Christ! This is the true bliss, the balm, which sweetens the pains and sorrows that are inseparable from the present life.

You will pardon me for being so bold as to state, in the first place, that you don't appear to me to be sufficiently advanced in inward experience to practice silent prayer for a long time. . . . I think it would be far, far better to combine ejaculatory prayer with silent prayer. Let forth such ejaculations as the following: "O my God, let me be wholly Thine!"—"Let me love Thee purely for Thyself, for Thou art infinitely lovely!"—"O my God, be Thou my ALL! Let everything else be as nothing to me!". . . But I think that such powerful ejaculations should be separated from each other, and intervened, if I may so express it, by short intervals of meditative silence. . . . And in this way you will be gradually forming and strengthening the important habit of silent prayer.

And this suggests yet another practical remark, too. When you are reading on religious subjects, you would do well to stop now and then for a few moments and betake yourself to meditation and prayer in silence; especially when any portion of what you read touches and deeply affects you. The object of this is to let the reading have its appropriate effect. Such reading will be very likely to edify and nourish the progress of the soul towards higher heights. The soul needs nourishment as well as the body. Its religious state, without something which is appropriate to its support, withers and decays.

Do not resort to severe austerities of self-inflicted mortifications. They may do for others, but surely not for you, as your feeble health does not allow for it. If you had a strong and sound body, and especially—which is the great point in connection with physical mortifications—if you allowed yourself to be ruled by your appetites, I should probably give different advice, but this is not the case.

But there is another mortification, madame, which I must earnestly recommend to you. Mortify whatever remains of your corrupt affections and your disorderly will. Mortify your peculiar tastes, your propensities, your personal inclinations. Among other things, learn to suffer with patience and resignation those frequent and severe pains which God sees fit to impose upon you. Learn also, from the motive of love to God, to suffer all that may happen of contradiction, ill manners, or negligence in those who serve you. In a word, mortify yourself by burying at all times, under a serenely even Christian temper, whatever thwarts the natural sensibilities; and thus place yourself in union and fellowship with the sufferings of Christ Himself. By taking these bitter remedies you will honor the cross once again. And especially if you mortify yourself and die, in your inward experience, to everything which is remarkable and showy. Learn the great lesson of becoming a little one, of becoming nothing. He does well who, in long fasting from things which the appetites improperly crave, lives upon mere bread and water; but he does better who, in fasting from his own desires and his own will, lives upon God's will alone. Let God provide all material as well as spiritual sustenance! This is what Saint Paul calls the circumcision of the heart.

I would advise you to receive the Eucharist as often as you conveniently can. Jesus Christ, who is presented to us in that ordinance, is the Bread of Life, which nourishes and quickens our souls. I shall not fail to remember you when I am worshiping before Him, greatly desiring as I do that He may set up His Heavenly Kingdom in your heart, and may reign and rule in you.

—J. M. B. de La Mothe Guyon

The calendar pages turned slowly during the months of incarceration in this place. Her only visitors were Monsieur Charon, Judge of the Ecclesiastical Court; Monsieur Pirot, a learned doctor from the Sorbonne University; and Father La Mothe, her half-brother. Several times these three came to ask Madame Guyon to make a signed confession of her alleged guilt. They wanted her to issue a retraction of her unorthodox religious views contained in her earlier writings. But each time she stubbornly refused to retract a single sentence. She would sooner die upon the scaffold, or remain imprisoned indefinitely, than utter the falsehoods they proposed. Once they brought a personal message from King Louis XIV himself in which he offered her immediate freedom provided she would grant permission for her young daughter to marry the Marquis of Chanvolon. Even to this she replied negatively; such a marriage, to a man who had so little Christianity in his principles and morals, would not be suitable for her Maria.

Unaccustomed to being refused, the King repeated his request, reinforcing it with the threat that she comply or spend the rest of her life rotting in prison until death would loose her bonds—or perhaps even be beheaded if she remained implacable. No doubt, if she had given in to his demands at this point no tragedy would have befallen her. But she would not betray her child by giving her over to such a man as the Marquis of Chanvolon. Neither would she be content to keep her relationship with the Lord Jesus Christ to herself. She did not want to risk offending the Lord in any way; nor did she want to better her situation at the expense of her daughter.

Little had Jeanne Marie de La Mothe realized that her childhood wish "to become a Christian martyr" would some day come so close to fruition. In her childish innocence she had foretold her own destiny: to be a Christian martyr—to give her life, if need be, for the cause of Christ and the gospel. Even as a child her desire was to please the Lord. Now, while sitting in her little room, shivering from the cold and dampness, or sweating from the hot rays of the sun from which there seemed to be no relief, Madame Guyon's thoughts often went back to that mere child of five who desired above all else to become a Christian martyr. Had that time already come? Would she be called upon to die for the cause of Christ?

· · · · ·

"In the times of the ancient law, there were several of the Lord's martyrs who suffered great hardship for asserting and trusting in the one true God. In the primitive church of Christ the martyrs shed their blood for maintaining the truth of Jesus Christ crucified. Now there are martyrs of the Holy Ghost, who suffer for their dependence on Him, for maintaining His reign in souls, and for being victims of the Divine Will.

"It is this Spirit which is to be poured out on all flesh, as says the Prophet Joel. The martyrs of Jesus Christ had been glorious martyrs, He having drunk up the confusion of that martyrdom; but the martyrs of the Holy Spirit are martyrs of reproach and ignominy. The Devil no more exercises his power against their faith or belief but directly attacks the dominion of the Holy Spirit, opposing His celestial motion in souls, and discharging his hatred on the bodies of those whose minds he cannot hurt. Oh, Holy Spirit, a Spirit of Love, let me ever be subjected to Thy will, and, as a leaf is moved before the invisible wind, so let me be moved by Thy Divine Breath; as the impetuous wind breaks all that resists it, so break Thou all that opposes Thy divine empire."

—Madame Jeanne Guyon

11

Freed—But Not Acquitted

Although Madame Guyon harbored no complaining spirit, her personal feelings were revealed with remarkable consistency in her correspondence. To a friend she wrote:

> I have just received your kind letter, and I can assure you that it has comforted me in my place of horrible exile. Sometimes I can apply to myself the expressions of the Psalmist: "Woe is me that I sojourn in Meshech, that I dwell in the tents of Kedar! My soul hath long dwelt with him that hateth peace." While I am kept here by the power of my mortal enemies, I can't help thinking of those who need spiritual instruction such as I can provide. What a mysterious providence it is which keeps me out of my place of labor, out of my element! It looks to me as if there were great numbers of children asking for bread, and that there is scarcely anyone to break it for them.

She longed to minister again as she had been privileged to do in so many villages and towns in France, Switzerland and Savoy. But she had no complaint. Instead, she thanked God for allowing her to correspond with so many from her restricted residence in the Convent of the Visitation of Saint Marie.

Four times during the eight months she was there, Monsieur Charon came with Monsieur Pirot to interrogate her anew. Polite and gracious as these gentlemen were towards her, they probed into her past and present views on religious subjects in an effort to determine the true depth of the nature of her beliefs and opinions.

"Is it true, Madame Guyon," asked Monsieur Pirot, "that when you went from Paris to Savoy, you went with Father La Combe as an associate and follower?"

"When I left Paris, monsieur, Father La Combe had not been in Paris for several years," she explained. "And, therefore, to have gone with him would have been an impossibility. No, no, monsieur, he was definitely not with me."

"Was La Combe instrumental in teaching you the doctrines of the inward life?" was Pirot's next piercing question.

Madame Guyon proceeded to tell how she had been taught the principles of her Christian faith in her early years, both in her parents' home and in the various convent schools she attended during her childhood. It was in 1671 that she first met Father La Combe, ten years before she went to Burgundy and Savoy. In his capacity as a visiting priest, Father La Combe came to the Guyon house as a spiritual director, being first introduced to her by her half-brother Father La Mothe.

Apparently Monsieur Pirot was under the impression that Father La Combe had participated in authoring Madame Guyon's book *A Short and Easy Method of Prayer,* which had caused such disputation among the clergy and was the primary cause of her present confinement. He was doing all he could to link Father LaCombe's name with her original manuscript in spite of her protest and denial.

"No, he did not, monsieur. I wrote that book myself while in Grenoble. Father La Combe wasn't even there at the time." Madame Guyon attempted to explain her position, knowing full well that no one was really listening to her. "I had no way of knowing then that this book would be printed. That was not my intention in writing it. A counselor in Grenoble saw the manuscript on my table. He examined it, and thinking it would be useful to others, he asked for my consent, which I readily gave, to have it published. It was his suggestion that I write the preface and divide it into chapters."

The interview went on and on. Monsieur Pirot and Monsieur Charon kept firing the same questions at her, over and over again, in an effort to trick her into a confession that more closely fitted their theories and accusations.

"From your book, are we to understand that you would disregard the use of the prescribed prayers of the Church? Even of the Lord's Prayer?" Pirot asked.

"Far from it. I have tried to explain the manner of using the Lord's Prayer more effectively. Yes, I have discounted the use of the Lord's Prayer and of all other prescribed prayers as a mere matter of rote— but for absolutely no other reason. It is not the repetition of prayers which renders us acceptable to God, but the possession of those dispositions of heart which the forms of prayer are intended to express." This was Madame Guyon's eloquent and heated reply.

Then Monsieur Pirot introduced a surprising piece of evidence: a letter which Madame Guyon claimed was an outright forgery. It was addressed to Father Francis of the Order of Minims. In this letter, Madame Guyon supposedly stated her determination to hold religious meetings in various private homes because it was too dangerous to hold them in her own house.

"By whom was this letter written?" inquired Monsieur Charon, nastily. "And what reason have you to think it is a forgery or a hoax?"

"I cannot speak of its authorship with certainty. But I do have my own opinions," she said. "This letter was laid before His Majesty King Louis, and it had a great influence in causing my imprisonment here. I suppose it was written by the scrivener Gautier, whose function in these transactions is known by me. This is not my handwriting, as can easily be proved if any cared to do so. Besides, it is addressed to Father Francis in Paris. It is a fact, and can be proven, that he left Paris for Amiens on the first of September. This letter is dated the thirtieth of October. The gentleman who has charge of educating my sons could assist me in obtaining proof on these particular points, if you are sincere in wishing to clear up this situation."

Continuing her response to Monsieur Pirot's series of questions about her religious opinions and writings, Madame Guyon stated, "I was born in the bosom of the Roman Catholic Church, as you well know. I was brought up in its principles, which I still love so dearly. It is hardly necessary for me to say that I make no pretensions to learning, as I am not a doctor of the Sorbonne. Yet it is true that I have sometimes uttered expressions which require theological emendation; and so I have already submitted myself to the correction of those within the Church who have the proper authority over me. I am ready to give my very life to the Church, but I wish to say that I am a Catholic in substance and spirit, not merely in form and letter. Truly, the Roman Catholic Church never intended that her children be dead in her forms; but rather that her forms be the expression of the spiritual life within them received through faith in Jesus Christ.

"In doing what I have done," she rambled (as one who has not had an intelligent conversation in many months is prone to do), "I had no expectation or desire of forming a separate party. But I wished to see the great principles of the inward life revived. It did not occur to me at all that I would ever be regarded as a heretic and a separatist. To declare me a heretic doesn't make me one! Truly I thought I might be permitted, in the sphere which Providence had assigned me, to labor for the revival of the work of God in the soul."

Nothing much seemed to come from all this questioning. The door to the outside world remained shut to Madame Guyon.

Then in October 1688, after eight long months of confinement in the Convent of the Visitation of

Saint Marie, Madame Guyon's cell door was suddenly flung open. She had an unexpected visitor. A messenger from the King entered.

"Are you Madame Jeanne Guyon? You are, are you not?" the soldier asked at once, not being accustomed to social amenities with a prisoner.

"Oui. Oui. I am Madame Guyon, monsieur," she replied, wondering what would come next. She was aware that many persons, even those of high rank, had been put into prison or killed for daring to express a view different from that sanctioned by the Church and the state. What other fate could she possibly expect?

"I have orders to release you immediately," he said, as he placed into her hand the official order of release bearing King Louis XIV's signature and seal. "You are free to go at once, madame," he intoned in a voice that reflected her new status of free citizen.

What wonderful news! Tears welled up within and overflowed her eyes. Praise for the Lord's unerring magnificence flowed from her like a torrential rain. Within a few minutes she gathered up her personal belongings and notebooks and regained her composure. Free at last! The day she had prayed for had come! But how could this be? Truly God had heard and answered her petition; He knew her innocence!

Upon stepping through the convent door into the fresh air and sunshine, Madame Guyon dropped to her knees, a free woman, saying, "Let me give thanks to Almighty God for His divine providence in liberating me."

Soon after retiring to the home of Madame de Miramion she learned that, in a sense, she had been ransomed by her friends. Her acquaintance with so many high-ranking society ladies proved to be God's means of affording liberation. Madame de Miramion had on one occasion been allowed to visit Madame Guyon at the convent, and as a result of this visit she had talked with other high-ranking, influential people about the terrible situation Madame Guyon was in and the injustice of it. She secured the backing and support of Madame de Maintenon, Madame de Maisonfort, the Duchess Beauvilliers and the Duchess Cheveuse to prevail upon the mercy of King Louis XIV in behalf of Madame Guyon.

A short time after her surprise release from the Convent of the the Visitation of Saint Marie, the Archbishop of Paris, who had been instrumental in her arrest and near conviction, came to Madame de Miramion's residence to suggest to Madame Guyon the less said about what took place during her commitment the better her lot would be. Madame Guyon assured him that he need have no concern. She held no hard feeling toward the Church officials, the nuns in charge of the convent where she had been kept those eight miserable months, or the King for allowing such an unjust thing to happen. She agreed to say nothing more.

Facts about Madame Guyon's family are rather scarce. She apparently had a closeness to her daughter, Maria Jeanne, who had married Monsieur L. Nicholas Fouquet, the Count de Vaux, during the time of Madame Guyon's incarceration. Because this son-in-law possessed a very understanding nature, Madame Guyon went to live with them for a while after her release, hoping to comprehend the new political climate in France.

Under the religio-political regime of such a personally ambitious and all-powerful ruler as King Louis the Great, as he was commonly called, the country went through a series of four major wars, extreme extravagance, and near financial bankruptcy of a most ruinous nature. King Louis XIV wanted to rule supreme in Europe. He hoped to conquer all the land west of the Rhine River, but was stopped repeatedly by military alliances between England, Spain and the Holy Roman Empire, along with other European nations. For the political advantage it would give him, King Louis XIV was desirous of winning the personal favor of Pope Innocent XII, the highest authority of the Roman Catholic Church. He aimed to make every French citizen and resident "Catholic or else!" To do this it was necessary to change the existing French law which expressly granted a measure of religious freedom to the people. So it was that in 1685 he revoked the Edict of Nantes, made in 1598 by King Henry IV, which had extended tolerance and legal protection to French Protestants and freethinkers for almost a century. Now, by government decree, any display of piety which could be judged as heresy became a crime against the state. The slightest deviation from strict Roman Catholic orthodoxy was punishable by exile, imprisonment or, sometimes, even death.

Legislation became more repressive under the

zealous influence of Father La Chaise, spiritual advisor to the King, and the influence of Madame de Maintenon. Edicts directed primarily against the French Huguenots were very severe indeed. Persons found guilty of heresy could be beheaded. Both priests and Protestant pastors were removed forcibly from their churches. Many priests were excommunicated and banished to convents, monasteries and prisons. Religious assemblies were prohibited except within the recognized Roman Catholic Church, its various religious orders and institutions. Protestant books and Bibles, along with the Psalter, were absolutely forbidden to be read and, if found, were confiscated and burned by the local authorities acting on behalf of Church and state. The singing of psalms was prohibited in private homes, in religious assemblies and in public places. These were but a few of the restrictions imposed upon the French people during Louis XIV's reign which forced people back into the grasp of the Roman Catholic Church and caused others to go to prison or to live in fear for their lives.

This same year, at the insistence of Father La Chaise, King Louis XIV of France urged Pope Innocent XII to proceed against Molinos's teachings, which the Jesuits regarded as perilous to Roman Catholic tradition. They were afraid that Molinos's ideas would open the way for the rapid advance of Protestantism. Michael de Molinos of Spain was at that moment confined in a Dominican monastery, having been condemned by a papal order. This man had counseled monks and nuns to serve God inwardly, to discard rosaries and religious relics, and to pray to God directly rather than through the intercession of the approved saints. Although Madame Guyon had no direct acquaintance with Molinos, they did share many of the same doctrinal views and opinions on religious matters. For this reason, the Jesuits singled out Madame Guyon as an alleged heretic like the condemned Molinos.

Both she and Molinos had been strongly motivated in their faith by the writings of Saint Francis de Sales, John of the Cross, Saint Theresa, Madame Jane Frances de Chantal, the Apostolic Fathers and Christian mystics like Augustine and Thomas Aquinas. Their principal teaching was simply that the Christian life is one in which inward peace, piety, and resignation to God's divine will make a life of commitment and service to the Lord Jesus Christ possible. But this was different from what was being projected by the official Church; and with King Louis XIV so determined to win a place in the Pope's favor, nothing so deviant could be tolerated.

In his attempt to bring everyone back into the good graces of the Church, the King went so far as to resort to military force and the point of a sword at a man's throat. However, the King's official decrees and harsh threats of arrest were not sufficient to make all the French Huguenots and other Protestants turn back to Roman Catholicism. This savage means of persuasion proved more effective in making Christian martyrs than Catholic converts.

Persons accused of being heretics were condemned by the Church and imprisoned as prisoners of the state. Some, without benefit of trial, were confined to monasteries and convents while their cases were supposedly under investigation. Many whose way of worship differed from that of the Roman Catholic faith, with its ritual and its tradition, were executed for their beliefs; others died from the inhumane conditions existing in the prisons at that time. In just the year 1687 alone, 147 Huguenots and others of equally non-orthodox persuasions, such as Jansenists, were sent to the Bastille; in 1689 sixty-one were so fated. The times were tumultuous indeed.

As the mass exodus of some two hundred thousand Frenchmen took place, France's economy was reduced almost to a level of national bankruptcy. In fleeing for their lives, the Huguenots picked up what few possessions they could carry and crossed the French border into Switzerland, Germany, Holland or England, where they hoped to find religious freedom, a freedom no longer attainable in their homeland. Since the Huguenots were mostly middle class— the most productive and prosperous people in the country—their departure in such large numbers tremendously reduced the amount of revenue to be collected by the French government. France was impoverished not only by this direct loss but by the discouragement and the prostration of energy of the harassed citizens who remained behind.

Finally, when even military force could not bring these people back into Roman Catholicism, the King decided to change his strategy. He had to do something to impress the Pope and thus elevate himself in his eyes. Besides, he had to save his country from an economic depression before it enfeebled France any more than it had already done.

Perhaps, the King concluded, some distinguished clergymen could accomplish this job of making New Catholics—better than all his legal decrees, military force, and threats of imprisonment and execution. So King Louis XIV looked around for a personable and understanding priest. He sought someone who would be loyal to the cause, would establish good rapport with the people, would be sympathetic enough of Protestants to win their confidence and would be politically ambitious enough to see what he could gain by succeeding effectively in his assignment.

About this time a young priest, Father Francois de Salignac de la Mothe Fenelon, was coming to prominence both within the Roman Catholic Church and in French political circles. Well recommended by His Superior, Father Fenelon seemed to possess the desired abilities to work successfully with Protestants. He also seemed ambitious enough to desire to attain recognition for his work in the Church and in the King's Court. So King Louis XIV agreed with his advisors that this Father Fenelon was ideally suited for the job.

The younger son of Count Pons de Salignac, Father Francois Fenelon was born in the Castle of Fenelon in Perigord, Sarlot, in southern France, in 1651. His early schooling took place mostly at home. As a youth he became fascinated with religion and the ways of the Church. When he was twelve years old he went to the University of Cahors and later to the College of Plessis in Paris, where he was an exceptional student. He preached his first sermon at the age of fifteen and went on to study theology at the Seminary of Saint Sulpice. Some of Father Fenelon's religious thinking and his sincere consecration to God must have come from the influence of Abbe Tronson, the Principal at Saint Sulpice Seminary. Abbe Tronson is classed by the Church as a great Christian mystic. In 1675, at the age of twenty-four, Francois Fenelon became an ordained Jesuit priest. For three years he served the Saint Sulpice parish as a most effective and dearly loved pastor. At one time he was quite serious about being called as a missionary to Canada, which was then under French rule. But because his uncle objected, Fenelon went back to his study of theology, philosophy, education and personal devotions. As it developed, Fenelon's real talent was writing and teaching. Some of his books on philosophy, education, and devotional subjects are prized even today among religious scholars.

Thus Father Francois Fenelon was assigned by King Louis XIV to minister among the French Huguenots, other Protestants, and New Catholics in the predominantly Protestant community of Poitou, France. However, before accepting the position, Father Fenelon requested that the King remove the soldiers from his diocese and give him freedom to employ more constructive methods in dealing with these people.

While serving God and country in Poitou, he heard about an unusual woman, a Madame Jeanne Guyon, a widow whose volunteer missionary work in Switzerland, Savoy and France was well-known among both Catholics and Protestants. Father Fenelon determined to make her acquaintance at the first opportune moment. Of course, he recognized how risky this was. Even a slight acquaintance with this young widow, a woman once accused of heresy, could cost him the King's fickle favor, and his reputation and political future would be destroyed. There was even the possibility of his being proclaimed a heretic by mere association with her; this a clergyman of his position could certainly not afford. Yet it seemed that nothing could turn him away from contacting this woman. But he knew he had to be cautious.

Late in October 1688, Father Fenelon had occasion to pass through Montargis, Madame Guyon's home town, on his return from his three-year assignment in Poitou. As discretely as possible, he made inquiry about Madame Guyon. Through the Duchess of Charost, a mutual acquaintance, arrangements were made for their first meeting at the Duchess's palatial home at Beine. Presumably Father Fenelon and Madame Guyon knew very little about each other prior to this. Whether or not this curious priest was familiar with her writings, we do not know; but her unique spiritual experience and total commitment to the will of God—of these he had heard much. And these two did have some things in common. Both came from extremely wealthy and noble families. Both were a part of high society and were well acquainted with the King's Court. Both were perceptive and intellectually deep. And, most importantly, both desired to know and to do God's will above all else.

Well under forty himself, Father Fenelon, with his kind ways, keen mind, charm and enthusiasm, had his career still ahead of him. He presented himself well no matter what the particular occasion, be it at an orphanage or in the King's Court. He was tall, thin, yet well-built, with pale complexion, rather large nose and deep-set eyes. At one and the same moment this man could be described as being solemn and serious, imaginative, curious and jovial, a devout and dedicated Christian and an intellectual giant in his time. Creative and original in his thinking, Father Fenelon exhibited a simplicity that made him resemble a prophet with the persuasive powers of an eloquent speaker. For that he was. His Superiors saw him as a man wholly dedicated to live and work for the glory of God, France, and the Roman Catholic Church.

. . . . .

After leaving the Convent of the Visitation of Saint Marie, Madame Guyon penned this letter to her younger brother, Gregoire Boivieres de La Mothe:

"My dear brother, it is always with the greatest pleasure that I receive any tidings from you; but your last letter gave me far more satisfaction than any previous one ever did. As you are the only surviving member of our family who appears to understand the dealings of God with me, and to appreciate totally my situation, I received your letter as a testimonial of your Christian sympathy.

"The Lord has seen fit to bless me much in the labors for a revival of inward religion; especially in Grenoble, where the work was very wonderful.

"I speak to you, my dear brother, without any reserve whatsoever. And, in the first place, my soul, as it seems to me, is united to God in such a manner that my own will is entirely lost in the Divine Will. I live, therefore, as well as I can express it, out of myself . . . in union with God. . . . It is thus that God, by His sanctifying, all-knowing grace, has become to me ALL in ALL. The self which once troubled me is eradicated and I find it no more. And thus, God being made known in things or events—which is the only way in which that 'I Am' or Infinite Existence can be made known—everything becomes, in a certain sense, God to me. I find God in everything which is, and in everything which comes to pass. The creature is nothing: God is ALL.

"And if you ask why it is that the Lord has seen fit to bless me in my labors, it is because He was first; and by taking away my own will He made me a nothing in the void. And in recognizing the hand of the Lord, I think I may well speak of God's agency physically as well as mentally, since He has sustained me in my poor state of health and in my trying physical weakness. Weak as I have been, He has consistently enabled me to talk in the day and to write in the night, over a long period of my life.

"After the labors of the day, I have, for some time past, spent a portion of the night in writing commentaries on the Scriptures. I began this at Grenoble; and though my labors were many and my health was poor, the Lord enabled me in the course of six months to write on all the books of the Old Testament.

"I am willing, in this as in all other things, to commit all to God, both in doing and suffering. To my mind, it is the height of blessedness to cease from our own action in order that God may act in us.

"And this statement, my dear brother, expresses my own particular condition, as it is my prayer that it may express yours. In such a state, riches and poverty, and sorrow and joy, and life and death are all the same: transient before the Infinite God. In such a state is the true heavenly rest, the true Paradise of the Spirit. . . ."

—Jeanne Marie B. de La Mothe Guyon

12

Meeting with Father Fenelon

No one could have known that the meeting be-tween Madame Jeanne Guyon and Father Francois Fenelon would be the start of a relationship with a tragic ending. Father Fenelon's distinguished career would be ruined, and many innocent Christians would endure years of persecution and imprisonment for their association with Madame Guyon.

Wearing his black cassock, relieved only by the white of his stock at the neck, Father Fenelon greeted the still youthful widow with his customary courtesy and charm. As for Madame Guyon, she had only recently come out of the Convent of the Visitation of Saint Marie. Now she was resting serenely at Madame de Miramion's home, pondering her next command from the Lord. She wore her usual stiff black dress, with a hood like a nun's fastened together under her dimpled chin, making her look demure and rather attractive in spite of her pock-marked face, the reminder of her bout with small-pox years before.

Both appeared to be intrigued with each other from the very first meeting. They talked at length, discussing the Holy Scriptures and such topics as the inward Christian experience, pure love, the Holy Spirit's work, and prayer. Father Fenelon, being a cautious priest, often objected to her more advanced theological statements. Madame Guyon endeavored to answer his questions with simplicity and with examples from the lives of the saints as well as from the Bible itself.

The priest went away impressed with all the spiritual insight and Biblical knowledge this woman possessed. The next day they met once again. This time, to avoid suspicion, they met at the home of the Duchess of Bethune in Paris. Madame Guyon again explained to this inquisitive priest the new spiritual life as she experienced it.

The following week, Madame Guyon could not throw off the burden she had growing within her for Father Fenelon's spiritual development. She fasted and prayed on his behalf. Then on this November 1688 weekend, she wrote to Father Fenelon, urging him to completely surrender his will to God: "For seven days past I have been in a state of continual prayer for you. I call it prayer, although the state of mind has been somewhat peculiar. I have desired nothing in particular. But my soul presenting continually its object before God, that God's will might be accomplished and God's greater glory might be manifested in it, has been like a lamp that burns in the darkness without ever ceasing for a second."

She went on to say in the letter: "The prayer

which I offer for you is not the work of the creature. It is not a prayer self-made, formal, or outward. It is the voice of the Holy Spirit uttering itself in the soul, an inward voice which man absolutely cannot prevent or control. The Holy Spirit prays with effect. When the inward voice ceases, it is a sign that the grace which has been supplicated has been sent down. I have been in this state of mind before for other souls, but never with such intense struggle of spirit and never for so long a time. God's designs will be accomplished upon you. I speak with confidence; but I think it cannot be otherwise."

Well-trained and educated in ecclesiastical matters, disciplined to act as if he knew the mind of God, this man could easily grasp spiritual concepts. This is evidenced by his summary of the highlights of Madame Guyon's *A Concise View of the Soul's Return to God and Its Reunion with Him.* This summary concludes that: (1) one must permanently give the soul totally to God, then bring all natural powers and appetites under its subjection; (2) one must quit relying on the pleasure of inward feelings; (3) one must not depend upon one's own ability, inward or outward; (4) one must fatalistically accept what comes; (5) one can then experience resurrection of the new life, the life of love; (6) finally, one can enter into perfect union with God.

However, it was some weeks before Father Fenelon fully accepted Madame Guyon's views as correct, abandoning his own, to enter into this deeper spiritual life experience for which his soul hungered so passionately. When he fully realized his need and

finally made a complete consecration and total subjection of his will to the will of God, his whole life
changed suddenly. Worldly desires and personal
ambition diminished in importance . . . all at once.
He became an example of Christ's holy love and
purpose. If anyone ever did put on the whole armor
of God, this man did after he was filled with the
Holy Spirit. Determined now to defend the faith
with God's weapons, Father Fenelon realized his te-
nets of faith no longer fully agreed with those of the
Pope—the dogmas set forth by the Roman Catholic
Church. From the day he first met Madame Guyon
he became a champion of Christian theology and
Bible doctrine, particularly the doctrine of death to
the self-life. Like any true soldier of the cross, before
long Father Fenelon discovered that he did, indeed,
have a spiritual enemy and a battle to fight for his
Lord by the power of the Holy Spirit.

Meanwhile, a particular decision was being made
that would secure Father Fenelon's rapid rise in political circles. The Duke of Beauvilliers, governor to
the grandson of the King, recommended Father
Francois Fenelon to King Louis XIV as a brilliant
scholar and outstanding religious educator who could
effectively tutor the young Duke of Burgundy, heir-
apparent to the throne, in interdisciplinary studies.
This was in August 1689. Since King Louis XIV was
already pleased with the way Fenelon had succeeded
in his work with Protestants and New Catholics in
Poitou, he did not hesitate for a moment to assign
Father Fenelon as tutor to his grandson.

In order to teach his young charge the duties of

his high office, Father Fenelon wrote *The Adventures of Telemachus*, a novel about a youth intimately observing the governments of many countries. His criticism of absolute monarchy, as he had stated clearly in correspondence to King Louis XIV, was tacitly implied in this book and his discussions with the boy. He also wrote *Fables* and *Dialogue*, which were stories designed to teach proper manners and acceptable behavior to the boy.

Headstrong, self-willed, temperamental and undisciplined, the young Duke was rightly described by those associated with him as "a rude ruffian of royal descent." After a time under the capable tutelage of Father Fenelon, the youth's attitude changed remarkably. He gained some self-control and self-discipline and began to display many good qualities—that must have come from the steady Christlike influence of Father Fenelon. In fact, historians claim that if the young Duke had lived to become the ruling monarch, most likely he would have been a very effective and just king, and the history of France would have embodied much less bloodshed.

Well-liked by the King, and with numerous friends in the King's Court, Father Fenelon had good reason to believe his ambition to minister permanently in the royal palace at Versailles would be reached without much manipulation. As spiritual director to many high-ranking persons he spent much time in the royal palace, which was his favorite place of ministry.

As early as 1697 Fenelon was appointed Archbishop of Cambray, where he was greatly loved and respected by the people. Clearly his star was rising rapidly.

"God kept me in such a disposition of total sacrifice that I was quite resigned to suffer everything, and to receive from His hand all that might befall me, since for me to offer in any way to vindicate myself would only be an insult to His infinite wisdom. When the Lord is willing to make anyone suffer, He permits even the most virtuous people to be readily blinded toward them; and I may confess that the persecution of the wicked is but little when compared with that of the servants of the Church, deceived and animated with a zeal which they think to be right. Many of these were now, by the artifices made use of, greatly imposed on in regard to me. I was represented to them in an odious light, as a strange creature. Since, therefore, I must, O my Lord, be conformable to Thee to please Thee, I set more value on my absolute humiliation and on seeing myself condemned by everybody than if I saw myself on the summit of honorable acclaim in the world. How often have I said, even in the bitterness of my heart, that I should be more afraid of one reproach of my conscience than of the bitter outcry and condemnation of all men!"

—Madame Jeanne Guyon

13

Bishop Bossuet's Opposition

During the first two years of Fenelon's association with Madame Guyon they met frequently at her daughter's pleasant new home, that of her husband Monsieur L. Nicholas Fouquet, the Count de Vaux. Father Fenelon was a close friend of the Fouquet family, so it was easy for him to see Madame Guyon there without drawing undue attention to his visits. In 1692, however, Madame Guyon left the Fouquet home and rented a modest private house in Paris. This enabled her to renew her friendship with the ladies in King Louis XIV's Court, where she saw Father Fenelon on many official occasions.

One of these ladies, Madame de Maintenon, was secretly married to the King after his wife, Marie Theresa, died in 1683. For political reasons their marriage was not publicly acknowledged as such. Madame de Maintenon had been the King's favorite mistress prior to their clandestine marriage. For many years King Louis XIV was France's absolute monarch, but the real controlling power behind the throne's major decisions, surprisingly enough, was Madame de Maintenon. She had the King wrapped around her little finger. She knew how to get what she wanted from him. Still, with all this attention, money and power, Madame de Maintenon had found no real happiness or satisfaction whatsoever. To a friend she wrote: "Do you not see that I am dying with utter melancholy, in a height of fortune which once my imagination could scarce have conceived but a short year ago? I have been young and beautiful, have had a high relish of pleasure, and have been the universal object of love. At a more advanced age I have spent many years in intellectual pleasures; I have at last risen to favor; but I protest to you, my dear madame, that every one of these conditions leaves in the mind a completely dismal vacuity."

So it was that when she needed a shoulder to lean upon, Madame de Maintenon sought the friendship of Madame Guyon and invited her to the royal palace at Versailles. They talked about the Blessed Savior's love, the remedy for sin, Christ's victory over the fallen nature and other Biblical truths. How Madame de Maintenon thrilled to find that faith in the Lord Jesus Christ could bring the knowledge of sins forgiven to her soul and real joy and happiness into her life! Where all else failed—Jesus never fails!

In 1686 Madame de Maintenon had established a charitable institution, Saint Cyr's Convent School, as a benevolent gesture to support and educate the daughters of persons who suffered losses or spent their lives in dedicated service to the state. Nearly two hundred and fifty girls under twenty years of age were enrolled in this boarding school. Generous contributions from Madame de Maintenon and other high-ranking ladies of the King's Court supported the school in all of its academic pursuits. Both Madame de la Maisonfort and Madame Miramion worked there regularly as instructors.

Granted unrestricted access to the school, Madame Guyon saw Madame de Maintenon there often. She devoted herself to counseling the girls on spiritual matters plus doing some teaching. After a time, some girls reported to Madame de Maintenon and Madame Miramion that Madame Guyon's counsel helped them to find God within themselves. This was a reality totally unknown by most of the girls prior to becoming acquainted with Madame Guyon. Although familiar with the rituals, forms, rigid discipline and traditional liturgy of the Roman Catholic Church, these girls heard, some for the first time, that Christianity is not just another religion but a way of living life to its fullest with Christ in the center. They came to know that God loved them, that His Son Jesus died to save them, and that He is risen from the dead to forever make intercession on their behalf to the Heavenly Father. As a result, a large-scale revival broke out at Saint Cyr's. The girls looked to Madame Guyon for spiritual help more than to the Mother Superior and the Bishop of Chartres, who served as chaplain to the institution. As the girls intently read the Bible, prayed and made vows to God, they witnessed to others about the Lord and how their lives changed abruptly for the better.

News about this revival spread to other communities. People came to confer with Madame Guyon as they had done in Gex, Thonon and Grenoble, where she had previously worked for the Lord. Although in rather poor health herself, Madame Guyon managed to talk and pray with all who came to her for spiritual guidance. Many people were converted. Some were miraculously restored to health after doctors had pronounced them incurable. Others found inner peace they had never known before. And so the revival went on!

Not far behind this outpouring of God's blessing came Madame Guyon's enemies, rapidly scattering lies, rumors and false accusations in an attempt to dissipate the good that had been done. As a result, the Bishop ordered her to cease working at Saint Cyr's Convent School.

That same year, early in 1689, some priests and theological teachers credited Madame Guyon with having begun, and having kept alive by her writings, the religious revival that broke out in the village of Dijon. Three years before, in 1686, Madame Guyon had stopped briefly in Dijon on her trip from Verceil to Paris. Father Claude Guillot was favorably impressed with her work; perhaps it was through his endorsement that her writings were so widely read in this town. In questioning local residents about their individual spiritual experiences and beliefs, the authorities discovered that some people's views tended to lean too much away from traditional Roman Catholicism. So when it was determined, or rather assumed, that Madame Guyon's book *A Short and Easy Method of Prayer* had generated this religious movement, and must have been responsible for what was called a heretical influence there, this group of priests and theological teachers set about to end the heresy as quickly as possible. They collected about three hundred copies of the book and burned them publicly amid great fanfare.

Such incidents did not stop Madame Guyon's desire to help souls find Jesus Christ. Wherever she went people came to confer with her. Revivals broke out right and left. Sincere persons like Sister Malin from Ham came, wanting to discover the truth of God's Word. Others, like Monsieur Peter Nicole, came not to benefit from her ministry but rather to attempt to convince her to return to the approved Roman Catholic doctrine and customs, and so get back in good standing with the Church. But she could not give up faith in the living Savior because she now knew that the reality of His presence in her life was not dependent upon confession, candles, and penances rightly performed.

Hoping there would be a cessation to the attacks triggered by Father La Mothe and Bishop D'Aranthon, Madame Guyon took refuge for several months in a small house on Fambourgh Street in Antoine, with only Monsieur Fouquet, the uncle of her son-in-law, knowing her whereabouts. She certainly wished to avoid imprisonment again, if such were possible. Soon the report circulated that Madame Guyon had disappeared from Paris and returned to the eastern provinces to teach her irregular doctrines there. This caused the authorities to look with suspicion into these areas, bringing persecution down upon local residents wherever there seemed to be a religious movement in progress. Because of this flowering climate of persecution, Madame Guyon decided to come out of hiding. In all good conscience she could not stay under cover while this happened. But, unfortunately, it was too late! Nothing she could do now could stop the strong, concerted opposition her half-brother and Bishop D'Aranthon of Geneva, along with Father Innocentius, Monsieur De Harlai, Monsieur Peter Nicole and Monsieur Boilear, had stirred up against her with such malice. These men and the Jesuits reported her every move to the authorities and were constantly demanding an investigation of her alleged heretical activities and influence.

The charges against Madame Guyon now reached the desk of Jacques Benigne Bossuet, Bishop of Meaux, a most zealous defender of the Roman Catholic faith. Because of the Bishop's thesis *A History of the Variations of the Doctrines of the Reformed Churches*, in which he subjected the teachings of Martin Luther and other reformers to severe scrutiny, Bishop Jacques Benigne Bossuet was regarded by Roman Catholics as an expert in judging heretical tendencies. Bishop Bossuet was determined to extinguish even the slightest glimmering of heresy that came under his jurisdiction. He agreed with the Jesuits in principle. But Bossuet's methods differed from theirs in that he used interrogation, debate, persuasive preaching and propagandizing to bring a person's erroneous views out in the open. Therefore he could not accept the Jesu-

its' resorting to direct opposition and persecution—
such as throwing rotten vegetables at a person, ston-
ing his house, following the accused person everywhere and preaching in the streets the fallacies of
his belief as a means of harassment.

Although Bossuet was eager to extinguish any
heretical deviation that came under his watchful eye,
he was hesitant and reluctant when it came to denouncing a woman publicly. It seemed inconceivable
to him that Madame Guyon, or any woman for that
matter, could produce such a heady stir in Paris,
Versailles and Grenoble that would be so very detri-
mental to the Church. Nevertheless, this woman was
accused of acts of heresy, sorcery and performing sa-
tanic magic, besides writing books and tracts of a
heretical nature. And he could not very well dis-
count the fact that stable men like the Duke of
Beauvilliers, the Duke of Chevreuse and Father
Francois Fenelon had come under this woman's influence and had been greatly affected and visibly
swayed by her teachings. However, except for these
reports and a pastoral letter from Bishop D'Aranthon
of Geneva, he did not actually know her.

A denunciation based on insufficient evidence,
he knew, would be most unfair and damaging, both
to Madame Guyon and himself. Thus it was that
Bishop Bossuet decided that until he could learn
more about Madame Jeanne Guyon firsthand he
would bide his time and do nothing . . . until he felt
certain—and then he would strike!

• • • • •

Writing now occupied much of Madame Guyon's

time. When she was not working on her manuscripts, she penned long, complicated letters to friends and acquaintances.

To one pastor she wrote: "The great thing to be kept in view by religious pastors at this present time is the complete distinction between outward or ceremonial religion and inward religion, or that of the heart. Religion, in its full development, is the same thing as the inward kingdom or the reign of God in the soul. And it is certain that this inward or spiritual reign can never be established by outward ceremonies and observances alone if divorced from the inner spiritual wellspring of God's divinity.

"The religion of the primitive disciples of Christ was characterized by being inward. It was the religion of the soul. The Savior made an announcement of unspeakable importance when He said, 'It is extremely expedient for you that I go away at this time: for if I go not away, the Comforter will not come unto you.' He seems to have intended by this announcement to turn their attention from outward things and to prepare their hearts fully to receive the fullness of the Holy Spirit, which He looked upon as the one thing necessary.

"The form is merely the sign of the thing. I may, perhaps, give offence in saying it, and am certainly liable to be misunderstood; but still it seems certain to me that there may be such a thing as outward praying—praying in the form but without the Spirit. It is true that the Savior gave a form of prayer, which is a very wonderful one indeed. Nevertheless, He rebuked long and ostentatious prayers, and disapproved of frequent repetitions. He tells the disciples that they are not heard for their much speaking, and assigns as a reason that their Heavenly Father knows what they want before they even ask Him. He says, 'When thou prayest, enter into thy closet, and pray to thy Father who seeth in secret, and thy Father who seeth in secret shall reward thee openly and fully.'

"Oh, sir, how much it is to be desired that *all* persons, getting beyond mere outward supports, may have their lives from God and in God! Such a day will certainly come to pass, I must state, however circumspectly I must do so. We see already some evidences of its approach in the lives of those who, in having no will but Christ's will, live by faith; whose whole joy is in having dispositions that are from God and with God, and who regard all outward things as the mere transient signs and incidents, and not the reality of life.

"It is with complete earnestness, therefore, that I adjure you, sir, to aid souls to the utmost of your powers in their spiritual progress, so that they may not stop short of God's inward reign. The subjection of human selfishness by holy love, and the subjection of the human will by union with the Divine Will, may be said to make Christ vibrate within us. Christ will come visibly in the silver clouds of heaven. But, in the spiritual sense, He may come *now*; He may come *today*, at *once* perhaps. Oh, let us labor for His present coming! Not for a Christ in the clouds, but for a Christ in the affections; not for a Christ seen, but for a Christ felt; not for a Christ outwardly represented, but for a Christ inwardly realized.

"On this subject it is difficult for me to express my free feelings, as they exist to an intensity rendering language inadequate to do justice to them. When will men renounce themselves that they may find God? Willingly, full willingly, I would shed my blood, I would lay down my life, if I could see the world seeking and bearing Christ's holy image.

"I remain yours in the Lord."

—Madame Jeanne Guyon

14

Under Suspicion of Heresy

In September 1693, Bishop Bossuet arranged with the Duke of Chevreuse, a long-time friend of both Madame Guyon and Father Fenelon, to visit her in Paris. Since Bossuet desired to gain insight and personal knowledge of this woman's religious views and spiritual experiences, he decided a face-to-face confrontation was necessary. Their first meeting ended with the Bishop acting upon Madame Guyon's suggestion to examine and evaluate, at his leisure, all of her writings.

Their second meeting took place on January 30, 1694. Being basically an honest man, Bishop Bossuet admitted he found nothing erroneous in either her book *A Short and Easy Method of Prayer* or in her *Bible Commentaries*. He spent most of three days plowing eagerly through her impressive life story, making notes as he went along on matters that needed further explanation from her own mouth. The rest of her writings, he said, would require a more thorough study. He felt the meaning of *The Torrents* was obscure and asked her for a written explanation, which Madame Guyon was able to supply. When it came to theological questions, she was most articulate. She also agreed to, and did, write a paper for him entitled *A Concise Apology for the Short Method of Prayer*, which was a detailed explanation of the book rather than a retraction.

A few weeks later another long conference took place at the home of Abbe Jannon, on Cassett Street near the Convent of the Daughters of the Holy Sacrament. Bishop Bossuet preferred to hold these meetings in complete secrecy. He did not want to be responsible for the Jesuits causing more trouble for Madame Guyon. Besides, there was the possibility that the accused might actually be innocent. So he went to great lengths to protect Madame Guyon from her enemies while his investigation of her writings continued. Since the Bishop was accustomed to dealing with books and sermons, argument and debate, he was apt to be imperious and abrupt when it came to understanding another's views. He spoke rapidly in well-thought-out phrases like a prosecuting attorney: "My dear madame, the doctrines which you advance involve the fact of an inward experience above the common experience of Christians, even those who have a reputation of holiness. When persons go so far as to speak of a love of God without regard to individual self, of the entire sanctification of the heart, and of impartation of the divine nature, have we not reason to fear there is some illusion? We are told that there is none that doeth good and sinneth not."

"There is no one except the Savior who has not sinned," agreed Madame Guyon as she went on to explain what she meant by sanctification of the heart and death to self. "There is no one who will not always be entirely unworthy of God's divine grace and mercy. Even when there is a heart which divine grace has corrected and rendered entirely upright, there may still be errors of perception and judgment—and this will render it necessary, therefore, to appeal continually to the blood of Christ for redemption. I cannot forget that we are required to be like Jesus; and that the Savior Himself has laid the injunction upon us to love God with all our heart and to be perfect as our Heavenly Father is perfect. My own experience has strengthened my convictions in this. I see no reason why I should deny the grace of God, which has wrought in me this one great salvation."

Madame Guyon answered like a trooper—which by this time she was, having suffered the indignity of such interrogation many times previously. Then Bishop Bossuet, discriminating as he was in his questioning, pointed out, "The Savior speaks in high terms of the man who went up into the temple and smote himself and said, 'Oh God, be merciful to me, a rank and low sinner!'"

"Very true, monsieur! This man was a sinner," she agreed. "But it is also true that he prayed to God to be merciful to him. And God, who is a patient hearer of prayers, granted his request with speedy mercy. Allow me to speak for myself—for my own Christian experience. I may say that I also have uttered the same prayer. I have smitten upon my bosom in deep anguish. Then deliverance did come, and I can say with extreme thanksgiving that my soul is now crowned with purity and inner peace."

Here Bishop Bossuet showed surprise at how well Madame Guyon managed to express herself and her feelings. He slowed down long enough to compliment her, saying there were few persons, least of all women, who could speak so fluently on theological subjects as she.

In many ways these two were well matched for a debate—with Bossuet schooled by the Church to be a skillful defender of the Roman Catholic faith, and Madame Guyon schooled by the Holy Spirit to be a living example of the faith she had found in Jesus Christ, the crucified and risen Savior she believed in and loved so fervently.

As the Bishop probed further, Madame Guyon responded quickly to his remarks. "What lack of faith! Men pray to God to be merciful, but they don't believe that He is willing to be merciful. Men pray for deliverance from sin and for sanctification, but they don't believe provision has been made for it. Thus they insult God. But tell me this: How can a man like you who has studied the Holy Scriptures so long and so profitably doubt the rich provisions of the gospel and deny that the many saints of the Church have been sanctified? I really can't understand your position."

"I don't deny that the doctrine of sanctification, when properly taught, is an acceptable doctrine of the Church," the Bishop retorted. "Neither can I forget the many rich examples we have . . . in Saint Francis de Sales, Saint Theresa, and Catherine of Genoa. But where is this spiritual blessing in the individual case? The evidence of sanctification should be very noticeable. This, you will admit, is a proper precaution. So allowing the general truth of the doctrine of sanctification and conceding that the promises of God are adequate to these results, I must still make inquiries with serious doubts into some of its aspects as presented in your particular writings, my good lady."

Like ammunition spit from a Gatling gun, Bossuet's questions kept coming. The session lasted through the afternoon and far into the evening, leaving Madame Guyon no time to rest. Many deeply religious subjects were discussed as Bishop Bossuet continued to probe further into Madame Guyon's reasoning and faith.

"Is it a mark of Christian lowliness to disregard principles and practices of the Church which have been sanctioned by the proven wisdom and piety of many ages?" the Bishop asked, referring here to the practice of self-inflicted punishment. "In your book *A Short and Easy Method of Prayer* you seem to imply that the austerities and mortifications of the flesh practiced in the Church are not necessary. What do you say in response to this?"

He stood there demanding an answer, having risen dramatically to the full height of his six-foot frame in doing so.

Madame Guyon patiently explained her present view on the subject. "Physical sufferings and mortifications which tend to bring the appetites into subjection are of great value. They are a part of God's discipline. I sincerely believe that. But they should not be self-sought or self-inflicted. They should be received and submitted to as they come in God's providence."

"I ask you another thing, Madame Guyon. Is it consistent with true lowliness of spirit to set forth the principle, as you've done in *The Torrents*, that souls in the highest religious state may approach the Sacramental Communion and partake of the sacred elements without any special preparation by the established Church?"

Allowing no opportunity for a reply, Bossuet went on. He wiped his perspiring brow. He, too, was tired from this long inquiry session. He had read and studied Madame Guyon's writings thoroughly, comparing every expression with the traditional teachings of the Roman Catholic Church, attempting to locate and sift out any hint of heresy. This was the job he had dedicated himself to do—and he would accomplish it!

"Understand," he proclaimed as he continued, "I have no desire other than to ascertain what is true. My job is to judge if there is heresy in your views. I do not object to the doctrine of Christian perfection or of pure love, or whatever other name may be given to it, in its general form, but I have serious objections to particular views and forms of expression sometimes connected with it. I find in your writings odious modes of expression which strike me as peculiar, to say the least. You say that to the sanctified soul everything which exists, with the exception of sin, is God. How mistaken can you be?"

Aware that her explanation did not please the Bishop at all, Madame Guyon asked for his candid

and charitable interpretation as she patiently pointed out the fact that the doctrine of sanctification is
sometimes erroneously represented by the imper-
fection of language itself. Madame Guyon was skillful and practiced in presenting her own defense when
she felt she was right, and quick to acknowledge
where she might have been wrong.

Then Bossuet raised another question. "You
sometimes speak as if the will of God, as well as
outward events, were identical with God Himself.
This can be misunderstood and, in point of fact,
such a statement is not strictly true. We use the
term "God" as denoting the whole of God, His intellect and affections, as well as His manifest will.
So to speak of the will of God, which is but a part,
as identical with God, which is the whole, is entirely erroneous and misleading indeed, and I am
sure now that I am not misconstruing your remarks."

To defend her own statement, Madame Guyon
agreed to the correctness of the Bishop's remark. "But,
while I make this concession, I am still inclined to
say that practically and religiously we may accept
the will of God as being God Himself, not only without doing wrong but with some benefits. We can
more easily make a distinction between God and
His power, and between God and His wisdom, than
between God and His will, if you follow my logic.
The will or purpose of God, in a given case, neces-
sarily includes something more than the mere act of
willing: it includes all that God thinks in the case,
and all that God feels in the case. How can you
possibly separate the two?"

"And I must confess," she went on, "that the will of God brings out, in my mind, more distinctly and fully the idea and presence and fullness of God than anything else. This is so much the case that, whenever I meet with the will of God, I feel that I meet personally with God. Whenever I unite with the will of God, I feel that I unite with God. So, although I am aware that a certain difference exists philosophically, God and the will of God are to me one and the same. He who is in perfect harmony with the will of God is as much in harmony with God Himself as it is possible for anybody to be."

Then, in another attempt to put her down, Bishop Bossuet threw out yet another trick opinion. "Inasmuch as women, like yourself, are not in a position to go through a course of theological education, it has sometimes seemed to me that it would be well for them to dispense with public service and missionary endeavors entirely. How can the blind lead the blind?"

Admitting that the lack of such qualifications had already caused her some perplexity, she offered in her defense her belief that God had called her and given her a message to give to her followers. "In God's great wisdom He sometimes makes use of feeble instruments; and I have thought, as He condescended, on one occasion at least, to use a dumb animal to speak His truth, He might sometimes make use of a woman for the same purpose."

She actually blushed upon making this reply. This was not the first time her call and ministry had been questioned because of her sex.

Hastily apologizing for his remark about women in the ministry, but by no means regretting having made it, Bishop Bossuet went on to enumerate further his objections to certain points, especially the idea of a spiritual experience that unites the soul so entirely with God as was stressed and developed in her writings. He confessed that the distinctions she had made and the explanations she had given him seemed to be reasonable and satisfactory, but somewhat irregular and totally unknown to him from his theological study and research or from his personal experimentation.

"I hope, monsieur, that you will not misunderstand when I say that I regret that you find it necessary to speak of this lack of personal experience," replied Madame Guyon. "The theology of the head is often obscure and uncertain, without the interpretation of the far higher theology of the heart which overrides the intellect. The head sometimes errs; but a right heart, never!"

Offended by this woman's remarks, the Bishop raised his voice in heated justification of his own Christian experience. After all, he had not risen from a novice to a bishop by being a heathen!

"Madame Guyon," he said, "I hope that I have experienced something of the grace of God. But I am free to acknowledge that I have not arrived at what you, and other writers who sympathize with your views, call the 'fixed state.' Is it possible that anyone can believe that Christians, however devout they may be, will arrive at the fixed state in this life—a state where there are not vicissitudes and where there is perpetual sunshine?"

"No, no, no," replied Madame Guyon with a passion unusual for one so even-tempered. "All that is implied by this 'fixed' state is a state which, being reached, is comparatively firm—one which is based more upon principle than upon feeling, and that lives more by faith than emotion. Those who live by faith, who see God equally in the storm and in the sunshine, rejoice in both. They know exactly what I mean. And those who fall short can hardly fail to be perplexed."

Then Bossuet proposed another subject, that of prayer itself. "The Holy Scriptures command us to pray without ceasing. The Savior said, 'Ask, and ye shall receive; seek, and ye shall find; knock, and it shall be opened unto you.' It seems very clear to me from this that prayer is a thing not only of perpetual command but of perpetual obligation. It is not easy for me to understand what prayer is, unless it is specific. Your system of present sanctification and 'pure love' seems to exclude specific prayer requests."

"And suppose it was so—which is definitely not the case, I might add," Madame Guyon responded in sharp debating form. "Is that state of mind to be thought of lightly which does not ask for any particular thing? What's wrong with praying to the Lord this way? I do not ask for this or that. I have no desire or petition for anything in particular, but desire and choose for myself only what God desires and chooses for me. Can you not see? This is an expression of praise rather than one of petition. Then one can experience, in oneself, the complete fulfillment of those directions of the Savior: 'Wherefore take no thought, saying, What shall we eat? or, What shall we drink? or, Wherewithal shall we be clothed? Because your Heavenly Father knoweth that you have recurring need of all these things. But seek ye first the Kingdom of God and His righteousness; and all these things shall be added unto you. Take, therefore, no thought for the morrow; for the morrow shall take thought for the things of itself.'"

"If I understand you correctly," Bossuet said, "your soul rests. That is, your soul is satisfied with what it now has in God, and you have nothing more in particular to request of God."

It had been a long interview. After all his questioning, Bishop Bossuet was still undecided as to how to proceed. Therefore, passing the buck, he requested that King Louis XIV appoint an investigating commission to examine Madame Guyon.

Those appointed to serve on this commission were Bishop De Noailles of Chalons, who later became the Archbishop of Paris, Abbe Tronson, the Superior of Saint Sulpice Seminary, and Bishop Jacques Bossuet of Meaux, all highly trained churchmen in good standing both in the Church and in the King's Court. The loyalty of these men to the state was an established fact. At the same time they were, as clergymen, aware that God still reveals Himself and His will to persons individually. Judging what is heresy in religious matters was not an easy assignment for them. So it was in August 1694 that this commission began its investigation.

Besides interviewing Madame Guyon several

times, they reviewed her two printed books, her letters and notes, and her Bible commentary manuscripts. Like "a child of another world," as she called herself, she responded to the questions put to her with courage, soft words, smiles and patient prayer. Bishop Bossuet introduced as evidence in support of the heresy charge the written explanations Madame Guyon had prepared for him. Little did she know that her own words were going to stand against her.

Upon learning of the charge against this woman, Madame de Maintenon and other influential friends decided to petition King Louis XIV on her behalf. They wrote a document reminding the King of Madame Guyon's good intentions and charitable works, asking that this all-powerful ruler intervene directly so as to protect her from the strong accusations made against her. When Madame Guyon read the petition she said, "Although this paper is pleasing evidence of the kindness of those who shared in drawing it up, it gives me some degree of uneasiness. I doubt whether it is the will of God that I should be protected and vindicated in this manner. I am afraid lest I should be dependent upon a human arm, or too eager to be relieved from my burden which God in His wisdom has seen fit to impose."

Resigned as she was to accept whatever came as being the will of God, she requested that they not intercede for her in this matter, but rather leave her destiny entirely in the hands of God. To justify her views and opinions as being in accord with Church-approved writers, she spent the next fifty days laboriously compiling a collection of quotations from authors whose views were similar to hers. This lengthy thesis, *Justifications of the Doctrine of Madame Guyon*, quoted Greek and Latin Fathers, Saint Dionysius, Saint Bernard, John Climacus, Catherine of Genoa, John of the Cross, Saint Theresa, Henry Suso, Thomas à Kempis, Gerson, Ruysbroke, Thauler, John de S. Samson, Harphius, Blosium, and Ruis de Montoya among others, and no doubt would have balanced the scale on her side if Bishop Bossuet had permitted the other commission members to read it into the commission proceedings. But he did not.

In her testimony, Madame Guyon reminded the commission that, since many of her writings were done before Michael de Molinos of Spain was condemned as a heretic by papal order, there was no reason at that time to feel cautious about expressing one's innermost religious thoughts and emotions. How could she possibly anticipate that her writings would cause such a furor? In fact, she did not even have publication in mind when she wrote these manuscripts. Now that that man Molinos was condemned by the Church, even the plainest statements used by writers of religious books were distrusted and regarded with suspicion.

The investigation proved nothing conclusive. There appeared to be no reason why the case was not closed, except that one commission member held out for a guilty verdict. Not satisfied with either an acquittal or a dismissal, the one opposing member, Bishop Bossuet, proposed that the commission remain in session until the case be resolved to his satisfaction. In the meantime, he suggested that

Madame Guyon voluntarily enter a convent in his diocese so he would have the opportunity to become better acquainted with her and make a more in depth study of her opinions.

Without hesitation Madame Guyon submitted herself to the authority of the Church as represented by this investigative commission. Although she knew this would not be the most conducive atmosphere in which to work, she agreed to stay temporarily at the Convent of Saint Mary in Meaux, with the understanding that she was free to leave when she pleased. She and her maidservant, Mademoiselle La Gautiere, went willingly at Bossuet's suggestion, expecting to stay perhaps three months while the commission completed its work.

While enroute to Meaux, some twenty-five miles northeast of Paris, that January 1695, the coach became stuck in the deep snow. The two women waited patiently with the driver, resigned to God's will even if it meant freezing to death in a snowbank. Both women came down with colds and coughing after this ordeal. In spite of this illness, Bishop Bossuet still insisted on questioning her almost daily. Madame Guyon had hoped her enemies would be satisfied once and for all. But, unfortunately, persecution and harassment continued even within the convent walls.

Bishop Bossuet came one day after her recovery with his *Pastoral Ordinance and Letter*, in which he condemned many prevalent religious errors rather strongly. He asked her to sign it. Knowing full well what this would imply, she curtly refused. She did, however, write a few words as a postscript. She expressed her desire to know and teach the truth and stated her readiness to submit herself to the decisions of the Church, whatever they were. In a later interview Bishop Bossuet demanded that she sign a more detailed confession. When she refused to do so, he threatened excommunication or permanent confinement if she did not accede to his demands. He always sneered now in her presence, since he knew he had the upper hand. He was determined to show this woman up as the heretic he believed she was.

"All I can say is, if you don't sign what I require, I will come with witnesses; and having admonished you before them, I will inform the Church of you, and we will cut you off as we are directed to do in Matthew's Gospel," Bishop Bossuet declared loudly.

His remarks were overheard by the Prioress of the Convent and some other nuns. "Why should you persecute this woman so much?" they asked.

To this he protested, saying the so-called persecution was not his doing at all. He claimed that, because of political pressure brought about by her enemies, his threats were necessary and justifiable. In other words, he had to get her written confession to protect his own position. It was beginning to be evident that under this priestly garment was a cruel, cynical man who allowed his political allegiance to affect his religious thinking.

On March 10, 1695, the commission completed its work. In condemning her accumulated writings, the commission members claimed that, according to their findings, thirty of her propositions leaned toward Protestantism and were, obviously, doctrinally in error. Her writings were declared unacceptable to the Church and directly bordering on heresy.

About a month later Madame Guyon signed a revocation, but not an admission of error. Then Bishop Bossuet gave her a certificate of orthodoxy to put her in good standing with the Church again. But a few days later, a dispute came up between them. Bossuet demanded the certificate be returned to him in exchange for a more explicit one which he had already prepared. But Madame Guyon wisely chose not to part with this original certificate which she knew was proof of her innocence. After this incident the Bishop left the convent, red-faced and practically fuming at the ears. He summed her up as "an arrogant woman with limited knowledge, whose merit was slight, whose illusion was palpable." But he and the other ecclesiastics who opposed her had to acknowledge that there was something almost uncanny about this Madame Guyon and her religious prowess nonetheless.

After six months of voluntary residency in the Convent of Saint Mary at Meaux, Madame Guyon and her maidservant decided to leave. On July 8, 1695, some friends, the Duchess of Mortemar and her daughter, Madame de Morstein, took them to the Fouquet home where they stayed with Madame Guyon's daughter, the Countess de Vaux. A few weeks later they moved into a private house, trying for a time to avoid all unnecessary contact with the outside world. Meanwhile, the opposition against

Madame Guyon was increasing geometrically, as more people became aware of her situation. Charges of heresy were made against her again. The Paris police now had orders to locate and arrest both Madame Guyon and her maidservant, who apparently shared the same religious views.

Once again a crisis was at hand.

• • • • •

Here sweetly forgetting and wholly forgot,
    By the world and the turbulent throng,
The birds and the streams lend me many a note,
    That aids meditation and song.

Ye desolate scenes, to your solitude lead,
    My life I in praise employ,
And scarce know the source of the tears that I shed,
    Whether springing from sorrow or joy.
Though awfully silent, and shaggy, and rude,
    I am charm'd with the peace ye afford;
Your shades are a temple where none will intrude—
    The abode of my Lover and Lord.

Ah! send me not back to the race of mankind,
    Perversely by folly beguiled;
For where in the crowds I have left shall I find
    The spirit and heart of a child?

Here let me, though fix'd in a desert, be free,
    A little one, whom they despise;
Though lost to the world, if in union with Thee,
    I am holy, and happy, and wise.

                              —Madame Jeanne Guyon

15

Again in Prison

It looked as if the snow would keep falling indefinitely. It was bitterly cold. Snow had been coming down for hours when Monsieur de Grez, an officer of the King's Court, arrived at Madame Guyon's residence with orders for her arrest. *A miserable day— it goes well with this miserable job,* Monsieur de Grez thought, as he stomped the snow off his boots.

Inside the house Madame Guyon lay on her bed, sick from fatigue and high fever. Monsieur de Grez hesitated to take this sick woman out in such dreadfully cold weather, so he decided to place both Madame Guyon and her maidservant, Mademoiselle La Gautiere, under house arrest until it would be more convenient to move them to the Castle of Vincennes as expressly ordered by the King.

Because of Madame de Maintenon's friendship with Madame Guyon, King Louis XIV was reluctant to send her to prison. He considered a convent sufficient as a place of custody for a woman, but the political pressure exerted by her enemies finally forced him to sentence these two women to a state prison. Of such significance was their arrest that the Marquis of Dangeaux, keeping a chronicle of the King's

Court from 1684 to 1720, deliberately mentioned it at length: "1696, Jan. 20th—The King caused Madame Guyon to be arrested a few days ago and sent her to the Castle of Vincennes, where she will be strictly guarded for an indefinite time. She is accused of having maintained, both by word of mouth and by her writings, a very dangerous doctrine—one which borders on heresy. She had imposed upon many persons of eminent virtue. A long search was made for her, before she was taken. She was found in Fambourgh Street, Antoine, in great concealment and fear for her safety."

A short entry in Madame Guyon's autobiography shows that, although she had turned down all of Madame de Maintenon's help, she was greatly disappointed by this most recent turn of events. She wrote: "All creatures seemed to be completely against me. I could only say these words: 'My God, my God, why hast Thou forsaken me?' I then put myself directly on the side of God, against myself."

Thus it was that Madame Guyon and her maidservant officially began their life as political prisoners, on December 31, 1695, in the Castle of Vincennes, a military and state prison located in the dense forest of Vincennes, near Paris. Many other persons were arrested and imprisoned also, victims of a widespread repressive drive put into motion at the King's command to free France from religious deviates considered by the Roman Catholic Church as leaning toward or favoring Protestantism.

Occasionally, Monsieur de La Reine, Chief of the Paris police, would interrogate those prisoners accused of being heretics concerning points of doctrine, certain expressions used in religious writings, and their present views on religious matters. However, being in prison, under constant guard, did not diminish the radiant joy of salvation in these women's lives. Together they passed their time singing songs of glorious praise to God. Her maidservant would memorize these songs as fast as Madame Guyon could compose them. Both were resigned to spending the rest of their days in prison until they would return to the Lord's bosom, if such was His will.

An entry in Madame Guyon's autobiography reflects this joyous attitude of resignation: "We together sang Thy praises, O my God! The stones of my prison looked in my eyes like rubies; I esteemed them more than all the brilliancies of a vain world. My heart was full of that joy which Thou givest to them who love Thee in the midst of their greatest crosses."

After a few tedious months, orders were issued and signed by the King, at the request of Archbishop De Noailles of Paris, transferring Madame Guyon and her maidservant to the Vaugirard Prison. On August 28, 1696, this transfer was accomplished under cover of darkness and in secrecy.

The prison at Vaugirard, a small village near Paris, apparently must have been connected with a monastery and a nunnery. Here the inmates had more liberty than at Vincennes. They could bring personal belongings with them and were encouraged to do something profitable with their time. Visits by family and friends were welcomed. They were also allowed to converse with other inmates and with their jailers. It was far more tolerable than at the Castle of Vincennes. These two women were thankful for small favors from the Lord, such as having access to writing paper, a stick pen, and ink made from soot mixed with water. So Madame Guyon was able to write long letters and work by the hour on her *Bible Commentaries*. She even corresponded with high officials, including Father La Chaise, the spiritual director to the King himself.

With the freedom to talk with the nuns in this place, Madame Guyon's desire to help other souls increased by leaps and bounds. She sought, by the power of the Holy Spirit, to inspire the nuns to find greater satisfaction in their religious vocation through a new spiritual relationship with the Lord Jesus Christ. As soon as the Archbishop of Paris heard how this woman was influencing the nuns and how God was blessing those residing and working within these convent-prison walls, he considered it an urgent priority to put an end to Madame Guyon's activities at once. In order to subdue this religious fanaticism, as he called it, before the matter came to the attention of the King, he came to Vaugirard on October 9, 1696, insisting that Madame Guyon sign an agreement to stop indoctrinating the nuns with her erroneous teachings immediately. She signed the form and promised to accept spiritual direction from Monsieur Lachetardier, the Curate at the Seminary of Saint Sulpice, mostly to save the nuns from further disciplines. Upon the recommendation of the Archbishop of Paris, Madame Guyon was restricted in all activities and denied visitors except with her spiritual director's written permission.

For most of 1696 and 1697, there was hardly a lull in the battle waged so bitterly by Bishop Jacques Bossuet against this frail woman. As guardian of the Church, the Bishop was charged to fight against what he considered to be heresy wherever it manifested itself. Defending the Roman Catholic Church and its dogma, as handed down by the Holy See, was his one objective; in fact, it was almost an obsession with him. He left no stone unturned and no word unsaid in his fanatic determination to rid his diocese of all allegedly dangerous and erroneous doctrines. Bossuet believed himself right, no matter what means he employed against deviates from the truth— as many in positions of power are prone to do.

There was little or nothing Madame Guyon could do to defend herself against his cruel attacks when she was confined to the Vaugirard Prison. Yet Bossuet would not let her be. He wrote pastoral ordinances and preached sermons against her. He ordered her books burned publicly.

At this time, the recently appointed Archbishop Francois Fenelon of Cambray, one of Madame Guyon's most devoted, long-time friends, took up the gauntlet on her behalf, as he could not condone such virulent attacks against one rendered as helpless as she. Of course, both of these men were masters of the pulpit—eloquent and forceful speakers. But Bossuet, famed for his ability as a debater, had the advantage of twenty years in age and experience over Fenelon. Bossuet spoke and wrote with the confidence of a learned teacher; Fenelon used a conversational-type presentation, as if talking with a group of friends. In attacking these irregular doctrines as set forth in Madame Guyon's writings, Bishop Bossuet knew he would win the high esteem of King Louis XIV, who wanted desperately to win favor with the Pope. He was also aware that such notice of him on behalf of the Church and the state would benefit his career tremendously. On the other hand, Archbishop Fenelon knew that his part in this controversy put him in dire jeopardy, personally and career-wise, once the knowledge spread concerning his "meddlesome" propensities. Yet he was prepared to defend those doctrines and views which he was convinced were in full accord with the Holy Scriptures and sanctioned by opinions expressed by many Church-approved writers. So it was that these two great minds locked in verbal combat in a controversy that—as the sparks flew between them—drew public interest from the far corners of the land.

After an eight-month study, Bishop Bossuet wrote and had published a remarkably scholarly book, a lengthy thesis entitled *Instructions on the State of Prayer*. In this profound and eloquent treatise he condemned Madame Guyon's teachings, impuned her character, and systematically attempted to discredit her widely circulated *A Short and Easy Method of Prayer*. The Bishop's book was actually begun in 1695 when Madame Guyon and her maidservant were residents of the Convent of Saint Mary at Meaux, but he did not have it published until 1697 because he had wanted to secure Archbishop Fenelon's approval of it before he acted.

Upon reading the manuscript, however, Fenelon stated in no uncertain terms that he could not in good conscience approve a book containing such slanderous implications relating to Madame Guyon's character without harming his own. So he withheld his approval. But this did not stop the angry and determined Bishop Bossuet from going ahead with its publication anyway.

Then, without mentioning Madame Guyon's name, Archbishop Fenelon tried in his book *Maxims of the Saints* to prove that doctrinal views concerning inward religious experiences were in accord with accepted dogma and were not new to Roman Catholicism. By quoting ancient Church council decisions he showed that the greatest and most spiritual giants, including John of the Cross, Saint Francis de Sales, Saint Francis of Assisi, Father Alvarez, Thomas Aquinas, Saint Bernard, Saint Theresa, Dionysius the Areopagite and Gregory Lopez, believed and taught this inner life of self-crucifixion, pure love, sanctification and Christian perfection just as did Madame Guyon. With the publication of this paper, all eyes turned toward the illustrious Archbishop. Besides corresponding with high-ranking and influential churchmen and statesmen, Fenelon wrote another long thesis entitled *An Answer to the History of Quietism*, in which he sought to show that there was nothing amiss in Madame Guyon's spiritual experiences and revelations from the Holy Spirit.

In attempting to refute Fenelon's *Maxims of the Saints*, Bishop Bossuet wrote two extremely controversial articles: *Traditionary History of the New Mystics* and *A Memoir of the Bishop of Meaux*. His other writings relating to this great controversy within the Church were *An Answer to Four Letters of the Archbishop of Cambray* and *A Summary of the Doctrine of the Archbishop of Cambray*, in both French and Latin. Two more of Bossuet's works appeared only in Latin, thereby limiting their circulation to the clergy. These were *Mystici in Tuto* and *Schols in Tuto*.

As this battle of words progressed, political feelings rose heatedly against Archbishop Fenelon. Obviously the religious climate did not favor his thoughts any more than it did Madame Guyon's. Even the highest authority of the Roman Catholic Church, Pope Innocent XII, was brought into it by referral from Louis XIV, King of France. Six days after Bishop Bossuet's letter to the King came to the attention of Pope Innocent XII, Archbishop Fenelon lost his position in the King's Court. He was ordered to leave the royal palace at Versailles at once and to return to Cambray and stay within its diocese boundaries. Twenty-four hours after this order was issued, Fenelon was on his way. Saddened by this turn of events, Fenelon left Versailles, the place he dearly loved, never to return. Convinced as he was of Madame Guyon's innocence, he could not say he had erred in attempting to defend her cause. Apparently such an admission on his part would have eased things for him.

In December 1697, Fenelon wrote to Abbe de Chanterac that he could get back into the King's Court simply by acknowledging his error, but he refused to stoop to such a level. Yet he held on to the hope that perhaps he had not lost the King's favor altogether. Hurt and disillusioned, he remained faithful to his priestly calling and assigned duty as a parish priest.

This referral from the King put the Pope in an extremely difficult position. Politically, he just could not afford to offend the King of France by ignoring the matter. Neither could he, as the representative of Christ, bring himself to decide hastily an issue where the serious charge of heresy was involved. So in an attempt to appease the King, Pope Innocent XII appointed a twelve-man commission to examine Archbishop Fenelon's book *Maxims of the Saints* and give an opinion as to its alleged heretical nature. After twelve meetings the commission was still divided in its opinion. Then the Pope selected a congregation of Cardinals to examine the questionable book more carefully as to its theological content. They too, after twelve meetings, were unable to reach a conclusion. A new Congregation of Cardinals was appointed. It may seem hard to believe, but after meeting no less than fifty-two times in regular session and several private-committee conferences, the result of their long deliberation was that a strong papal decree was issued on March 12, 1699, condemning twenty-three propositions from the *Maxims of the Saints*.

It was quite obvious that this action from Rome was merely a political maneuver to save face. No one knew how to break this dilemma which had been thrust upon the Pope. No true judgment on the doctrinal views expressed in Fenelon's book was ever given. Although the committee condemned twenty-three propositions, not one of the Cardinals outrightly condemned the content of the book itself. Nevertheless, Bishop Bossuet assumed that he was victor over the discredited Archbishop Fenelon in their long argument over Madame Guyon's allegedly irregular doctrines.

. . . . .

Love constitutes my crime;
 For this they keep me here,
Imprison'd thus so long a time
 For Him I hold so dear;
And yet I am, as when I came,
The subject of this holy flame.

How can I better grow?
 How from my own heart fly?
Those who imprison me should know
 True love can never die.
Yea, tread and crush it with disdain,
And it will live and burn again.

And am I then to blame?
 He's always in my sight;
And having once inspired the flame,
 He always keeps it bright.
For this they smite me and reprove,
Because I cannot cease to love.
What power shall dim its ray,
 Dropt burning from above?
Eternal life shall ne'er decay;
 God is the life of love.
And when its source of life is o'er,
And only then, 'twill shine no more.

    —Madame Jeanne Guyon

16

Persecution Grows

Without a shadow of a doubt, Madame Jeanne Guyon was one of Christ's most shining witnesses within seventeenth century Roman Catholicism. She moved among the rich and high-ranking as freely as among the poor. Her unique ability to influence others on spiritual matters, uncanny as it was, caused most of her trouble with both the state and the Church. Some of France's most renowned people were touched by her ministry of God's Word and came to her defense, but they were unable to aid her effectively. Dukes and duchesses, princesses and nobles—even Madame de Maintenon, the mistress and later secret wife of King Louis XIV—came to know Jesus Christ and His great salvation because of Madame Guyon's concern for souls.

Madame Guyon is widely acclaimed today. Her name has gone down in the annals of religious history as a mystic, one of the Quietists, a prolific writer and one of few persons in the history of the world to have attained such a fabulously high degree of spirituality. The conviction that God is ALL in ALL carried over into absolutely every phase of her life and impelled her to talk about Jesus Christ constantly.

It was this profound conviction that caused Madame Guyon and thousands of other devout Christians, both Catholic and Protestant, to be caught in the religio-political situation in France that brought persecution upon all whose religious sentiments differed ever so slightly from the established and approved doctrines and traditions of the Roman Catholic Church.

When the spring of 1698 arrived, Madame Guyon was still in her Vaugirard Prison confines. One day two gentlemen of immaculate demeanor, elegantly dressed in rich clerical robes, visited Madame Guyon's small and modest living quarters in the prison where she had been kept for almost two years now. One was the Archbishop De Noailles of Paris, a kind and compassionate man who had been responsible for her transfer from the Castle of Vincennes to Vaugirard. The other was her appointed spiritual director Monsieur Lachetardier, the Curate of Saint Sulpice Seminary, who came to see her rather frequently. They brought a letter which they claimed was written by her old friend Father La Combe.

In this letter Father La Combe urged Madame Guyon to repent of her irregular doctrine and make a full confession of her transgressions against the Church. Dubious as to the authenticity of such a document, and being innocent of these gross allegations, Madame Guyon would not acknowledge its receipt and flatly refused to believe it had been written by La Combe's hand. Furthermore, she would not confess anything that might be used to support the serious heresy charges against her.

Apparently her enemies, namely the sly Bishop Bossuet and her cunning half-brother Father La Mothe, used these priests in a devious scheme intended to discredit her even further. For years she had faced harassment, persecution, false accusations and finally prison itself because of her personal consecration to God. Nothing but the love of God and the power of the Holy Spirit could have enabled this woman to endure such treatment. For in spite of the immediate situation and deprivation imposed upon her, Madame Guyon's Christian testimony remained steadfast. She had no doubts about her Blessed Lord. "Who, then, shall separate me from the love of God?" she wrote in her autobiography. "Neither persecutions, nor prisons, neither men or devils— nor anything else." Through it all, she remained supremely confident that God loved her and was everywhere present with her in His omnipotent wisdom.

Already persecution and severe difficulties had fallen upon many who were in any way associated with Madame Guyon, especially Father La Combe and Archbishop Fenelon. If they had been capable of looking into the future they would have seen that their troubles were only beginning, with the worst yet to come.

In 1696 Monsieur Godet Marais, Bishop of Chartres, issued an *Ecclesiastical Ordinance* condemning Madame Guyon's writings as false, rash, impious, heretical in nature, and tending to revive and propagate the errors of Martin Luther, John Calvin and other reformers. He went so far as to have Saint Cyr's Convent School, where Madame Guyon had taught, searched for her books and for seditious correspondence and manuscripts belonging to Archbishop Fenelon. That same year the King also had Madame Guyon's son removed from public service as a lieutenant in the King's Guard, a position he had held for over two years. His record was good, therefore the reason for his dismissal could not have been his behavior as a soldier or a question of loyalty to the King. His dismissal had to be caused by the Church's controversy with his mother and nothing else.

Friends of Archbishop Fenelon were also suddenly, and without just cause, removed from their high-ranking positions in the King's Court. In the fall of 1697 the King himself questioned the Duke of Beauvilliers. Then in June 1698, Abbe Beaumont and Abbe de Longeron were, without warning, deprived of their titles of Subpreceptors and dismissed from the King's Court also.

Father La Combe had already been banished and later was imprisoned in the Bastille, as an advocate of Madame Guyon. Confinement in the Bastille proved too severe for him. Physical and mental anguish stripped him of his faculties. He was then transferred to a public insane asylum in Charenton, near Paris, where he drowned, a babbling, drooling idiot, in a pool of his own waste. What a pitiful end for a man of such brilliance and promise.

In September 1698 the "lettre de cachet" was delivered to the warden-priest in charge of Vaugirard Prison authorizing transfer of the fifty-year-old Ma-

dame Jeanne Guyon and her maidservant, Mademoiselle La Gautiere, to the Bastille, where political
prisoners were usually kept under the most outra-
geous conditions. The "lettre de cachet" bearing the
King's signature and seal was sufficient, even if secured secretly, to keep one imprisoned in the Bastille
indefinitely. Life here was the ultimate hell on earth,
as they were quick to discover.

· · · · ·

"It is owing to Thy goodness, O God, that there
now remains to me the prime consolation of having
sought and followed Thee faithfully, of having laid
myself upon the altar of sacrifice in the strength of
pure love, of having labored for Thine interests and
glory. In the commencement of my earthly existence, death and life seemed to combat together; but
life proved victorious over death. Oh, might I but
hope that in the conclusion of my being here on
earth, life will be forever victorious over death!
Doubtless it will be so, if Thou alone dost live fully
within me. O my God, who art at present my only
life, my only love, my Savior!"

—Madame Jeanne Guyon

17

Imprisoned in the Bastille

Like all Parisiennes Madame Guyon and her maid-servant must have looked with awe upon this imposing, four-story, gray stone prison-fortress many times as they passed by on foot or in a horse-drawn carriage. The great and dreaded Bastille, with its thick stone walls and high towers, took on even larger dimensions for these women when they realized they would soon be inside those walls to stay. It was not a pleasant thought.

Yes, every Frenchman had heard about this gruesome place. It had the reputation of being far worse than any other prison on the continent. In most instances, the mere possibility of imprisonment there for opposing either the Church or the state served as a deterrent to keep people in line. Only a few stubborn ones dared to speak out. A person convicted of a major crime in France at that time was simply beheaded, and so dealt with quickly. Those left to rot in cells and dungeons of state prisons were mostly thieves and minor criminals, excommunicated churchmen and priests, persons accused of heresy, and those who had offended the King in some manner.

Outwardly, the Bastille was an imposing structure. Built in the latter part of the fourteenth century as a fortress to defend the city of Paris from invading armies, the Bastille was used from the days of King Louis XIII (Louis XIV's father) and his prime minister Cardinal Richelieu as a place of ultimate incarceration for anyone who proved to be too troublesome to those comfortably ensconced in high places.

Eighty-foot towers, four-stories high, united by massive stone walls about twelve or thirteen feet thick, enclosed two large open courtyards. These courts were separated from one another by lower inside walls, placed strategically to curtail movement within. The entire building was surrounded by a deep, wide moat with a guarded drawbridge. At the base of each tower was a below-ground dungeon. These dungeon cells were almost totally dark and poorly ventilated by one small window. Above the dungeons rose, successively, four prison apartments, or cells, in the form of irregular polygons, measuring approximately eighteen feet across at the widest place and about eighteen feet from floor to ceiling. An occupant could exercise only by walking back and forth across the small confines of the room. The top cell was somewhat smaller.

The towers had names and the cells were all numbered. It was actually impossible to see either the ground or the open sky from inside these prison cells because the twelve-foot thickness of the wall at the top of the tower increased until at the ground level the wall was about eighteen or twenty feet thick. Each cell-apartment had one small window, open to the weather in all seasons. Both window and chimney had heavy iron grates set in the stone casing to prevent the escape of prisoners. The three-inch-thick doors, made of two layers of oak planking, were equipped with locks and heavy bars. The floors were laid out with rough stone tile. Each cell contained essentially the same furniture and major accommodations—a bed which was little more than a straw pallet, a blanket, a wooden table, a chair or bench, a wash basin, an earthen water pitcher, a commode jar, a candlestick and a straw broom. They had neither stove nor fireplace; just a tinder box was provided for heat against the cruel Parisian winter. One cannot imagine how cold such a place could be. The slimy dampness would chill a person to the bone for sure.

When a prisoner came to the Bastille, his name was recorded in the registry book with the date of arrival and the name of the tower and cell number that was assigned to him. From then on he was identified simply as "Number One in Tower du Tresor" or "Number Two in Tower de la Comte." This way curious jailer-guards had no way to learn the prisoner's real identity. Once in the Bastille, everything was taken from a prisoner except a little clothing and a few absolutely essential personal items: a comb and a Bible, a prayer book, rosary or crucifix perhaps. Regardless of the person's rank or the nature of his crime, whether rich or poor, everyone was treated in the same hellish manner—without regard for human dignity.

Upon her arrival at the Bastille, Madame Guyon

was escorted brusquely by a jailer-guard to her cell. It was a far cry from the elegance she had once been accustomed to in years gone by. Weak, sick and exhausted, she found her straw pallet in the darkness and lay down to sleep. It was miserable. Repulsive odors and noises in the corridor kept her awake. She tossed restlessly throughout the night. Her flesh protested against such an environment. Bedbugs, lice, spiders and rats were her constant companions. As bad as Vaugirard Prison or the Castle of Vincennes were, they were like a country estate compared to this wretched place. Here prisoners did their own laundry and housekeeping. It took a long time to dry clothes in these dark, damp cells. In time the garments and blankets wore thin and afforded very little warmth at all. The cells were extremely hot, muggy and smelly in the summer—cold, wet and slimy in the winter. Smoke from bonfires in the open courtyard below and foul odors from the putrified moat and sewerage outside added to the already deplorable conditions. With no sanitary facilities, poor ventilation, polluted water and spoiled, putrid food, it was no wonder many suffered from fever, nausea, diarrhea, insect bites, rashes and running body sores. When too sick to do laundry, eat or even sweep the floor, the prisoner—no matter who he was—had to lay in his own filth, vomit and excreta, unattended for weeks on end. Live or die, there was no one who cared.

About sunrise the guards banged on the doors shouting, "Get off your soft beds! Do you loafers expect to sleep all day?"

Buckets of food were distributed from cell to cell

twice daily. Meals usually consisted of moldy bread, cabbage and cold chunks of meat. Sometimes they had mutton and soggy bread crusts with a cup of sour wine. A person had to dip his hands into the bucket to pick up the food. Anything left over was put back in the larder and served the next time around. A lady of refinement like Madame Guyon would, no doubt, imagine herself to be a poorly treated barn-yard animal at feeding time when food had to be eaten in such a deplorable and degrading manner.

One of the greatest dangers to face here besides filthy conditions was the monotony of everyday existence itself. Inactivity, boredom and possible insanity were ever-present hazards prisoners had to face. Some people are reported to have trained rats and spiders, their constant companions, in order to have something to occupy their waking moments, trying to overcome this lack of activity. Days seemed endless. Nights even longer.

Madame Guyon kept her mind busy by communicating inwardly with God, singing songs of praise and thanksgiving like the Apostle Paul and Silas when they were in prison. She spent hours praying for her enemies' souls and for the other prisoners whom she had no opportunity to meet, except for a glimpse once in a while of a person going past her barred door with a guard. She began an acquaintance with the rats who frequented her cell and began praying for their freedom, too, as they also had the misfortune to be so incarcerated.

A few months after these two women entered the Bastille, the report filtered out via the grapevine that the notorious Madame Guyon had died. But it was not true. It was her faithful maidservant who had died. The poor girl could not endure such deprivation. The mistaken identity was easily understood. Since prisoners were identified to the jailer-guards only by tower name and cell number, their real names were not generally known. Someone may have heard that Madame Guyon was in the Bastille and so may have assumed that this other woman prisoner so much in love with the Blessed Savior was the once wealthy widow of Monsieur Jacques Guyon. Because of their close association since the beginning of Madame Guyon's widowhood, they were oftentimes taken for one another anyway. They had gone through a great deal together in many places, including Gex, Thonon, Grenoble, Paris, and in and out of convents and prisons. This maidservant had remained with little Marie Jeanne Guyon in the Ursuline Convent at Thonon while Madame Guyon carried on her ministry for the Lord in that neighborhood. It had become her deep inner conviction that God required her to stay with Madame Guyon. She felt that since it was a blessing to have personal acquaintance with this godly woman, it was an honor to share in her extreme sufferings and hardship. Even though the state authorities made dire threats and Church officials offered promises of absolution to her, in their combined efforts to persuade her to speak up against Madame Guyon, Madamoiselle La Gautiere never betrayed her employer and benefactor for even one heartbeat.

Madamoiselle La Gautiere once wrote to a friend:

"Is it not enough to say that she was an instrument in the hands of God to bring me to a working knowledge of Himself—that God whom I now love, and whom I shall love forever? She taught me the great lesson of self-denial, of dying to the life of nature, and of living only to the will of God. I never can forget the patient diligence she used, the sureness she exhibited, and the holy love which animated her on my behalf. So do not wonder that I love her. Yes, I love her because she loves the God that I love; and it is with a love which is real, living and operative. This love has the power of uniting our hearts in a manner which I am unable to express verbally; but it seems to me that it is the beginning of that union which we shall have in heaven, where the love of God will unite all in Him."

Although imprisoned, Madame Guyon was confident it could only be with God's permission that such a thing could happen to her. Shortly before entering the Bastille, she wrote to a close friend: "I feel no anxiety in view of what my enemies will do to me. I have no fear of anything but of being left totally to myself for extended time periods. So long as God is with me, neither imprisonment nor death will hold any real terrors. Fear not—if they should proceed to extremities, and should put me to death, come and see me die. Do as Mary Magdalen did, who never left Him that taught her the science of pure love."

So, in spite of the locked doors, the barred windows, the cold dungeon walls and all the personal discomfort and humiliation accorded her in prison, that inextinguishable joy and unmeasured spiritual freedom within this woman's soul rose toward heaven in voluminous praise—praise that could not be contained or explained except that she had found God to be vitally real. Her prayers, praise and tears, offered as acceptable sacrifices to the Lord, were as worthy before the throne of God as the highest Mass offered in the world's most gloriously adorned cathedral.

Somehow, while in the Bastille, Madame Guyon managed to obtain some sheets of paper and wrote several letters to high-ranking people and other acquaintances sympathetic toward her unfortunate plight. To one she wrote in detail about the gross injustice of the charge which had brought her to this dreadful place:

> I am said to be charged with being a hypocrite. But by what evidence is the charge supported? It is certainly a strange hypocrisy which voluntarily spends its life in undue suffering; which endures the cross in its various forms—the calumny, the poverty, the persecution, and every kind of affliction and humiliation—without reference to worldly advantages. I think one had never seen such a hypocrisy as this perpetrated before.
>
> Hypocrites have generally two objects in view: one is to acquire money, the other is to acquire popularity. If such are the leading elements involved in hypocrisy, I must do myself the justice to say that I disclaim any acquaintance with it. I call God to witness—that I absolutely would not have endured what it has been my lot to endure if by so doing I could have been made Empress of

the whole earth, or have been canonized while living. It was not earth but *God* that has called me to act as I do. I heard a voice which I could not disobey. I desired to please God alone; and I sought Him, not for what He might give me but only for Himself. I had rather die than do anything counter to His will manifest within me. This is the sentiment of my heart; a sentiment which no persecution, no trial, has made me alter.

Being accounted by everybody as a transgressor, I was made to walk in the path of my suffering Savior, who was condemned by the Sovereign Pontiff, by the Chief Priests, the doctors of the Law, and the judges deputed by the Romans. But the love of God rendered my sorrows sweet indeed. My purpose has remained unchanged. Happy are they who are sharers with Christ in suffering.

History records the fact that Madame Guyon spent four years in the Bastille in solitary confinement, shut away from human companionship and forbidden to see her family and friends. Even the consoling light of the sun was denied her by the huge prison walls themselves. Except for the jailer-guards and a confessor-priest, the only persons she saw during this time were those officials who came periodically to conduct required interrogations. Signing a confession of her supposed guilt would have been a simple matter that would have liberated her instantly. But not for one faltering moment would she consider doing such a thing! She would stay in prison until liberated by death itself, if need be, rather than to deny the Lord Jesus Christ's power unto salvation or to make retractions about her spiritual experience and belief.

Here was a woman so much in love with Jesus, so desirous to do what God would have her to do, that nothing could cause her to deny her Blessed Lord and Savior and the power of the Holy Spirit in her life.

Her autobiography contains only a short reference about the Bastille: "When things were carried to the greatest extremities, being then in the Bastille, I said, 'O, my God, if Thou art pleased to render me a new spectacle to men and angels, Thy holy will be done!'"

She also penned a short poem about her confinement. But she never said very much about what really happened inside those massive towers.

Whether Madame Guyon was abused or beaten at any time we do not know for sure. Certainly she must have suffered extreme mental deprivation, personal humiliation and inhumane treatment. However, stories of what happened to those incarcerated in the Bastille were always frightening, even to one with faith in the living God. Many died. Those who survived and were later released were forbidden to talk about what took place between those massive stone walls—on the threat of being returned. All we know is that they usually looked like walking skeletons.

In 1702 she came up for review. Because of her failing health, Madame Guyon seemed to be on the verge of dying. So the authorities decided to release her to spend her remaining years in retirement with her son at Diziers, near Blois. Of course there were conditions connected with her release. She was ordered to remain with her son and not to communicate with anyone on religious matters or do anything to promote her irregular religious views.

Although only fifty-four years of age, she now appeared to be much older. She was pale and thin, anemic, with graying hair. Those four years in solitary confinement had taken their harsh toll upon her physical body. Exposure to extreme heat in summer, bitter cold in the winter, prolonged dampness and lack of direct sunshine, made her physical condition deteriorate rapidly. Several times she was believed to be near death, suffering without relief from recurrent fever, some cough, chilblains, faintness, fatigue, and swelling and numbness in her arms and legs. Perhaps she had pneumonia, rheumatism, arthritis or even tuberculosis. Due to her stoic beliefs, she was not one to complain. She did not fear death. It was just that she felt called to work for the Lord and was determined to live long enough to accomplish God's will.

When she had first set out on her mission to Switzerland, she was a wealthy young widow. Now her money was completely gone; her life spent. God had spoken. She had answered His call as best she could. Then years of persecution and prison followed. Now she was free once again! Although she came out of the Bastille with little of this world's goods, she was indeed rich in the mode of the Spirit.

• • • • •

Strong are the walls around me
That hold me all the day;
But they who thus have bound me

Cannot keep God away:
My very dungeon walls are dear,
Because the God I love is here.

They know, who thus oppress me,
    'Tis hard to be alone;
But know not, One can bless me
    Who comes through bars and stone:
He makes my dungeon's darkness bright,
And fills my bosom with delight.

Thy love, O God, restores me
    From sighs and tears to praise;
And deep my soul adores Thee,
    Nor thinks of time or place:
I ask no more, in good or ill,
But union with Thy holy will.

'Tis that which makes my treasure,
    'Tis that which brings me gain;
Converting woe to pleasure,
    And reaping joy with pain.
Oh, 'tis enough, whate'er befall,
To know that God is ALL in ALL.

                    —Madame Jeanne Guyon

18

Released at Last

When it became common knowledge that she was in her son's house near Blois, people came to her once again for spiritual help, advice and prayer, as they had previously. Her days of ministry apparently were not yet ended. In fact, her usefulness increased to the point that many people, including clergymen and nuns, came with their spiritual problems and Bible questions. She also corresponded with fellow Christians in France, Germany, Holland and England.

Of course, the Roman Catholic Church kept a close, watchful eye on Madame Guyon's whereabouts, as did her personal enemies. But the Church exerted no strong effort to prevent her from seeing people who came to visit her at Blois. This may have been due in part to the fact that Bishop Jacques Benigne Bossuet, the ardent defender of the Roman Catholic faith, died in 1704, and King Louis XIV, because of his failing health, was no longer as politically aggressive or interested in such matters. In 1715 his great-grandson, Louis XV, came to the throne at the age of five, with Philip, the Duke of Orleans, serving as regent.

Always thankful for God's faithfulness, Madame Guyon prayed for those who disliked her so strongly. Great was the spirit of forgiveness within her heart for all humanity regardless of how their evil ways affected her work for God. After her release from the Bastille she issued a statement that she held no bitter feelings against those who had caused her so much difficulty. Besides, she was still espoused to her Heavenly Bridegroom, the Lord Jesus Christ, and looked forward with great joy to that day when she would meet Him face to face in eternity.

During these later years, arrangements were made for the printing of her autobiography. This is an unusual volume of great inspiration, well worth reading.

One day word came to Blois that her faithful friend and defender Archbishop Francois Fenelon had suffered a fall from a horse. He did not recover, but died on January 7, 1715, at the age of sixty-five.

Their friendship had cost Fenelon almost everything he had ever wanted on the temporal plane. It also gave him the thing he needed most—the knowledge necessary to bring him into a close personal relationship with Christ, which all his early study and commitment to the priesthood had not quite done. This was Madame Guyon's one regret—that so many friends and innocent persons had suffered persecution, some becoming martyrs for Christ's sake, because of their close association with her.

On June 9, 1717, at the age of sixty-nine, fifteen years after her release from the Bastille, this "child of another world" went home at last—united with her Heavenly Bridegroom, the Lord Jesus Christ, in that better world.

She was buried in the Church of the Cordeliers at Blois, France, in a modest grave.

*   *   *   *   *

"IN THE NAME OF THE FATHER, SON AND HOLY GHOST.

"This is my last will and testament, which I request my executors, who are named within, to see so executed.

"It is to Thee, O Lord God, that I owe all things; and it is to Thee that I now surrender up all that I am. Do with me, O my God, whatsoever Thou pleasest. To Thee, in an act of irrevocable donation, I give up both my body and my soul, to be disposed of according to Thy will. Thou seest my nakedness and misery without Thee. Thou knowest that there is nothing in heaven or in earth that I desire but Thee alone. Within Thy hands, O God, I leave my soul, not relying for my salvation on any good that is in me, but solely on Thy mercies, and the merits and sufferings of my Lord Jesus Christ. . . ."

—Madame Jeanne Guyon

Bibliography

Bell, Herman F. and McFarland, Charles E., *Religion Through the Ages*. New York: Philosophical Library Publishers, 1948.

Bradford, Cameliel, *Daughters of Eve*. Cambridge, Massachusetts: The Riverside Press, Houghton Mifflin Co., 1930.

Catholic Encyclopedia, Vol. X. New York: Robert Appleton Co., 1914.

Day, Rt. Rev. Victor, D. G., *The Continuity of Religion (Bossuet)*. Helena, Montana: publisher not given, 1930.

de la Bedoyere, Michael, *The Archbishop and the Lady*. New York: Pantheon Press, 1956.

Encyclopedia of Religion and Ethics, Vol. IX. New York: Charles Scribner's and Sons, 1961.

Fenelon, Francois, *Christian Perfection*. New York: Harper and Row, 1947.

_____, *Let Go*. Springdale, Pennsylvania: Whitaker House, 1973.

Guyon, Jeanne M., *Madame Guyon, An Autobiography*. Chicago, Moody Press, n.d.

_____, *Experiencing the Depths of Jesus Christ*, Gene Edwards, Ed. Compton, California: Christian Books, Inc., 1976.

Jackson, Samuel M., Ed., *The New Schaff-Herzog Religious Encyclopedia*. Grand Rapids, Michigan: Baker Books, 1959.

Lawson, James Gilchrist, *Deeper Experiences of Famous Christians*. Anderson, Indiana: The Warner Press, 1911.

Prothero, Rowland E., *The Psalms in Human Life*. London and New York: Thomas Nelson and Sons, 1903.

Upham, Thomas G., *The Life and Religious Opinions of Madame Guyon*. London: Allenson and Co., Ltd., 1961.

Vos, Howard F., *Highlights of Church History*. Chicago: Moody Press, 1960.

This book was produced by CLC Publications. We hope it has been helpful to you in living the Christian life. CLC is a literature mission with ministry in over 50 countries worldwide. If you would like to know more about us, or are interested in opportunities to serve with a faith mission, we invite you to write to:

CLC Publications
P.O. Box 1449
Fort Washington, PA 19034